# POLICING IN MULTICULTURAL BRITAIN

Endearing
Linda
/
Musa Khan
Jalalzai
28/6/2012

# POLICING IN MULTICULTURAL BRITAIN

## Racism, Colours, Riots and Cyber Terrorism

Musa Khan Jalalzai

**Afghan Security Studies Ltd**
15 Farmingham Road, Tottenham, London, N17 0PP
Ph: 0044 7581279626. E-mail: Zai.musakhan222@gmail.com

Published by Afghan Security Studies Ltd
15 Farmingham Road, Tottenham, London, N17 0PP
Ph: 0044 7581279626. E-mail: Zai.musakhan222@gmail.com

Published in Great Britain 2012

Catalogue record for this book is available from the British Library

Policing in a Multicultural Britain: Racism, Colours, Riots and Cyber Terrorism by Musa Khan Jalalzai

**Afghan Security Studies Ltd** is a London based Small Company, founded in 2012..

Typeset and printed at Intype Libra Ltd, London

ISBN 978 0 9571615 0 4

# CONTENTS

CONTENTS

# INTRODUCTION

The failure of police and intelligence networks during the London riots, phone hacking scandals and the resignation of senior police officers from their posts put the credibility of the UK police and other law enforcement agencies in question. In August 2011, the UK Police Chiefs admitted that tactical mistakes allowed vandals to loot and destroy shops, houses and markets across the country. The issue of law and order has been a main topic of intellectual forums and newspapers since the London attacks in 2007. Institutional racism and lake of coordination among various policing and security agencies and the recent loot and burn game has been the centre of considerable attention for both government and communities since 2011.

Recently, hundred of police officers accused of misconduct and racist behaviour escaped punishment by quietly resigning from their posts, according to the BBC panorama investigation. More than four hundred eighty nine police officers from forty seven forces now face misconduct action, but majority of them allowed leaving through back door between 2008 and 2010.

Police Commander Peter Spindler recently admitted that his department will not allow corrupt officers playing with their powers in an illegal ways. In 2011, police allowed more than 130 employees to relinquish job instead of facing misconduct panel. According to official figures, more than 900 serving police officers have criminal record while Daily Mail reported at least 944 serving police officers found involve in illegal practices. *"The Metropolitan police, Britain's largest force, came top with 356 officers and 41 PCSOs with convictions"* the newspaper reported.

Policing experts understand that the basic cause of the involvement of police officers in crime is considered to be their frustration or insufficient salaries. Lake of social education also caused their intolerance or racism but generally speaking, the police needs to establish social education centres to meet the challenge. In my understanding, quantity is not important than quality of services. On Page 35, Independent Review of Police Officer and Staff Remuneration and Condition Report, Part-1 for 2011 has revealed the strength of the UK police and its related forces:

*"Since 1978, the size of the police service increased by an additional 35,500 police officers to a total of 143,734 in March 2010. These officers have also received increasing support from police staff, who have more than doubled in numbers in this period, to a total of 77,900 and a further 16,915 police community support officers . . . These national figures must be considered with an appreciation of the very substantial variation in the size of the work force of the 43 territorial police forces in England and Wales. As at March 2010, there were around 144,000 police officers in the police force of England and Wales, of which 11,000 were above the rank of sergeant."*

Notwithstanding the strength of the police force, according to a Home Office recent report, more than 200,000 people including children are missing every year. The causes of missing are well known. Some are vulnerable here, some are jobless, some are frustrated and some have become the victim of trafficking and prostitution. The UK police receive the reports of more than 360,000 missing people every year across the country. More interestingly, every year, some 12,000 individuals are reportedly missing from various health care centres.

On 4th August 2011, riots across the United Kingdom began with the murder of a black man Mark Duggan. He was killed by police in Ferry Lane, Tottenham Hale London. The riots spread to many areas and in the fight between the police and protesters, police reported 2175 injuries. There were attacks on the police and rescue services personnel, widespread burning and looting, in most affected areas, police begin to feel unsafe to confront the looters.

Police commanders and decision makers faced the consequences of tactical mistakes and weak decision making process—the two key elements that badly damaged the historical image of the UK police force. A recent private research report revealed that police officers had abandoned the streets and markets of London to looters due to the lake of coordination and communication system. We don't blame that police had willingly allowed robbers to loot shops and burn markets, but one thing is clear that either police was in frustration or the lake of equipments compelled them to retreat.

The Police National Information Centre had failed to respond effectively. Daily Mail reported the London Police Chief, Bernard Hogan saying that former police commander had failed to put enough police in the streets. Having supported my view of intelligence failure, Mr. Bernard told

MPs that tactics of the police were flawed while it needed to review intelligence infrastructure.

After an official inquiry report, more than 382 police officers were either dismissed or forced to resign. A government funded study recently revealed that majority of young people who took part in London riots were driven by a combination of excitement and police attitude. Vice Chairman of the Police Federation Simon Reed in his statement disclosed the fact that: *"The police are the public face of a criminal justice system that is failing and that's why we are being blamed."*

In August 2011, the looting and burning in the streets of Britain's big cities astonished the police department their efforts of maintaining law and order were washed away. Strategies used by the police and other law enforcement agencies failed and their way of tackling the crisis was severely criticised. The police lost its own credibility and trust of communities on the one hand and faced government criticism on the other. This kind of criticism on the police tactical mistakes and non-professional way of operation further put in lower position the moral of the force.

The controversial issue of policing in the UK was being discussed in forums and intellectual debated during the riots in 2011 that unless the police change its way of operation, they will further loose the trust of communities and government. According to the report of Internet Journal of Criminology (Black and Asian police officers and support staff: Prejudices, Identity, Agency and Social Cohesion, 2006):

*"One of the main motivation of the British government's movement away from the multiculturalists agenda is that it is now seen as too simplistic and to have contributed to too many inward looking and, therefore, economically disadvantaged communities."*

The Home Affairs Select Committee recently completed some inquiries into policing in the UK and focused on what is likely to be the key element of reforms. The committee finally published a comprehensive police and crime commissioner's report in December 2010. Home Secretary criticised the police chiefs for their handling of violence while police officers rejected the Prime Minister's decision to hire a former New York police chief as an adviser in the wake of the riots. These rivalries between the police officers and government Ministers raised many questions that the involvement of politics in policing may further exacerbate the crisis.

Another issue that widened the clefts between the police and government was the row over police funding and the need to surge so many officers onto the streets. The police clearly felt aggrieved that they had been criticised for the way they handled the riots. Institute for the Study of Civil Society London in its report, (The Public and the Police-2008) has criticized the way police operates:

*"The public have no power to influence policing. The public have no power to influence policing. All decisions are taken by politicians and their appointees, but there is no accountability within the system. Since the Police Act 1964 successive governments have accrued power to the centre. Centralization has led to politicization and the introduction of targets. Bonuses are paid to senior officers based on compliance with targets. Officers*

*are now classifying as crimes things that would previously have been dealt with informally or under a different classification."*

Communities complain about the inactive presence and invisible participation of police in streets and towns and demand that delivering policing—whether in form of force or service should not be based on discrimination. The day to day increasing distrust between communities and the police are matter of great concern not only for the government in power but for the Home Office and policing improvement agency. A new image of the London police appeared after the recent riots is considered to be contradictory as the police demonstrated inconsiderably.

The lack of institutional coordination and the present complex way of governance may create more economic and political problems in near future. Reform in the police and intelligence agencies is a constant need while government needs to focus on the domestic violent criminal culture and extremism instead of spending millions of pounds in tackling the threat of international terrorism. The UK may face more violence both in England and Northern Ireland in near future and Improvised Explosive Devices will be used in attacks on police forces.

To meet the challenges effectively, the government recently published a new version of its Counter-Terrorism Strategy, known as CONTEST. The aim of CONTEST is to reduce the risk of terrorism but the four strands called PPPP (*known as pursue, prevent, protect and prepare*) have not been too successful as violent clashes in Northern Ireland left many police officers injured in 2011.

In summer 2011, the re-launch of Britain's Counter

Terrorism Strategy (CONTEST) by Home Office to tackle violent radicalization, extremism and militant networks, received furious response from sectarian and extremist groups. Home Office claims that Part of CONTEST "Prevent" strategy which focuses on violent extremist tendencies, terror groups and youth radicalization, support vulnerable people and communities. Prevent was first introduced in 2007 as counter terrorism strategy, known as CONTEST. This is the best counter terrorism strategy and most effective instrument for the government, but unfortunately it faced an open hostility from Muslim extremist groups.

The Intelligence and Security Committee (ISC), in its annual report for 2010-2011, and the Joint Terrorism Analysis Centre (JTAC) warned that the threat of international terrorism was 'severe' but the strength of the terror and extremist networks is evident from the changing levels of security in the country. On 9 November 2010, Home Secretary announced a review of *'PREVENT'*, but terrorism experts criticised the newly updated prevent strategy as it does not reflect national security demands because in its recent debate, British parliament signalled the radicalisation of students in British universities.

Experts view PREVENT and the present security plan for Olympic 2012 as an ineffective because terror and extremist groups have developed very strong networks in both England and Northern Ireland, can easily disrupt the 2012 Olympic game. Religious fanatics and extremist from several states have an advance booking for the game and on their arrival, how the police and intelligence agencies can identify or counter their activities?

Cyber attacks during the Olympic game cannot be ruled out. National Security Strategy singles out the 2012 games as being at major risk. The London Olympic can come under attack from cyber terror networks based in UK. There will be a new and modern type of subversion, because more trained people are joining extremist network. More extremists are entering the country and more young people are being trained in terror camps of extremist outside the country. Small-scale attacks can lead to significant cascading failures in interconnected networked system. Cyber terrorism represents a bigger threat to the UK economy and military industry. In 2011, Computer Weekly.com reported Iain Lobban, the head of GCHQ, the UK's electronic spy agency, saying that more than 20,000 E-mails with malicious software were found on government networks each month, with more than 1,000 deliberately targeted them.

Cyber Security and the UK's Critical National Infrastructure, a Chatham House recent report (September-2011) warned about the increasing cyber attack on UK institutions. The report highlights cyber threat and warned that threat and vulnerability is mounting and that the public and private sectors are all under increasing pressure to do something about cyber security. Improvised Explosive Devices and other home-made bombs can be more effective weapon against the law enforcement agencies both in England and Northern Ireland.

**Musa Khan Jalalzai**
East London. UK
January 20 2012

# CHAPTER 1

## POLICE, COLOURS AND RACISM

While we walk down high streets in Britain, specifically, the streets of London, we normally come across different white, black, yellow, Asian white and British white colours with brown or black hair, turbans, small and big noses and red and blue skins. In reality, these colours represent Britain as a most beautiful country in Europe, but the multicultural policies of successive governments, that shaped the present contradictory image of British society, left significant impacts on the shifting identity definitions of white, yellow and black colours.

The United Kingdom has become increasingly diverse society, but the recent riots across the country created a wide-ranging social gap between the government and communities. In Northern Ireland and Scotland, specifically, sectarian conflict marked out the boundaries of community through religious identities. These sectarian identities are further exploited by political groups. Sectarian and political affiliations in these two provinces caused weakness of Britishness, emergence of hate culture, while some communities consider people of opposite sect as other.

This wrong way of ethnic and religious thinking in a

modern society like Britain raises many questions. Religious schools and their sectarian agenda to divide society on opposite directions is another problem causes instability. Sectarian mind is normally encouraged at home and mosques and reinforced at schools. Minorities are faced with fundamental dilemma and do not want to accept the norms of dominant white culture. They are practicing their own sects and religions in their own religious places; neither shares their values with British society nor wants to be involved in a joint community work. They don't want to mix their colours or values with the society they live in.

To mix these colours properly, government, NGOs and councils never paid immediate attention to the flawed process of social transformation, while no proper research has been carried out either by councils or state funded institutions to mend the clefts. In these circumstances, while we hear the depressing statements of British parliamentarians about the failed multiculturalism, radicalization, alienation and prevailing gang culture in the country, our dream of strong British society is vanished.

The United Kingdom is now not the country of twentieth century; the decline of Britishness, trust deficit, the eroded confidence in the police, councils and the scandals of phone-hacking badly damaged reputation of the country abroad. Last year, on British Parliament website, I read the article of Arabella Thorp and Steven Kennedy who have painted an irksome picture of British society in these words:

*"Drug abuse, violent crime, teenage delinquency, family breakdown, welfare dependency, poor urban environments, educational failure, poverty, the loss of traditional values, teenage*

*pregnancy, dysfunctional families, binge drinking, children who kill: all have been cited as proof that we have a broken society."*

Governments and social organizations often tried to constitute relations with immigrants in the context of post colonial discourse which resulted in a big social failure. Plans and policies of successive government to promote settlement of immigrants on the bases of ethnicity, race and religion created more problems. Prime Minister David Cameron recently warned that Britain's long standing policy of mixing the colours is a complete failure and responsible for fostering extremism. Extremist groups have established a strong network and now started challenging the police and other law enforcement agencies. They openly threat writers and journalists while the UK police have failed in protecting vulnerable people. The Prime Minister desperately said:

*"Under the doctrine of state multiculturalism, we have encouraged different cultures to live separate lives, we have failed to provide a vision of society to which they feel they want to belong. We have even tolerated these segregated communities behaving in ways that run completely counter to our values."* He said.

If we look at the contents of Britain social strategy, we will find out some draw-backs in the existing way of enforcing multiculturalism that probably hindering the process of integration. All the above mentioned policies and ways of mixing different colours into British society resulted in the fragmentation of society and moreover, jeopardized the future of diversity. The way of mixing colours may needs some amendments. Police is reluctant to take action against known criminal and extremist due to the fear of community reaction.

The most controversial role of the police and its inability to tackle criminal gangs further complicated social mixing program. Racism and discrimination in both the police department and Borough Councils have causes more social problems. Councils are not housing the right people. Recently, hundred of police officers accused of misconduct and racist behaviour escaped punishment by quietly resigning from their posts, according to the BBC panorama investigation. More than four hundred eighty nine police officers from forty seven forces now face misconduct action, but majority of them allowed leaving through back door between 2008 and 2010.

After an official enquiry report, more than 382 police officers were either dismissed or forced to resign. A government funded study recently revealed that majority of young people who took part in London riots were driven by a combination of excitement and police attitude. Vice Chairman of the Police Federation Simon Reed in his statement disclosed the fact that: *"The police are the public face of a criminal justice system that is failing and that's why we are being blamed."*

The UK Border Agency is doing differently and still not providing effective service citizens expect. Recently, UKBA lost data of some 124,000 migrant applications. According to the House of Commons Home Affairs Select Committee report, this is a big mistake, while immigration minister, Damian Green said that he inherited chaotic immigration system. Labour Party immigration spokesman, Chris Bryant criticized the failure at the heart of government. He complained that government is not paying proper attention to the performance of UK Border Agency.

Following the August 2011 riots, intelligence failure and the police non-professional way of operation, Prime Minister David Cameron asked Home Secretary to review the situation properly. The cross-government report, published on 1 November 2011 also recommended support to local areas to tackle the problem. Home Office in London recently launched an Organized Crime Strategy (01 August 2011) to profile organized criminals, disrupt their financial networks and establish a new organized crime coordination centre.

The Home Office plans to introduce the system of police and crime commissioner in all 43 police forces in May 2012, means the present system needs some changes after the police failure to tackle the riots professionally. To restore the confidence of public and business community, Home Office, Met and UKBA needs to modify their strategies of policing community.

## The death of multicultural society

Ethnic minorities, colours and diversity have made British society more colourful. These colours once played an important role in the country's economic and cultural development, but the present shapes of Britain's social and cultural diversity, prevailing criminal culture and institutional racism, have threatened national security and social cohesion. Criminal networks of European mafia groups have established their underground operational command in the UK and trying to criminalize the country economy and financial market. They are deeply involved in serious organised crime business.

The invasion of professional criminal networks, violent extremists, unskilled labour, war criminals and drug mafia on British society from all sides has created a threatening environment, fear and insecurity. Investment opportunities are going to shrink. Population overcrowding and the pack of hundreds of thousands marooned and illiterate refugees on the thin and sensitive geographical body of the state have increased in economic, social, cultural and political problems.

The recent riots in which people from all ethnicities, colours, religions and cultures played their destructive role proved why Britain has traditionally been characterized as a failing multicultural society. There are communities, under-classes and groups of people locked in a cycle of deprivation, poverty and unemployment. Their political, social and economic isolation has dragged their children into the culture of gangs, organised crime, violence and teenage pregnancy. Children, raised in isolation by single mothers without fathers are becoming the victims of criminal gangs and drug mafia.

In August 2011, the looting and burning in the streets of Britain's big cities astonished the police department that all its efforts of maintaining law and order were washed away. Strategies used by the police and other law enforcement agencies failed and their way of tackling the crisis was severely criticised. The police lost its credibility and trust of the communities on the one hand and faced government criticism on the other. Intellectual circles started commenting on the failure of multiculturalism and diversity.

Social commentators termed as 'rubbish' the importance of multiculturalism after the statement made by the Prime Minister. Politicians pinpointed the erosion of traditional values and the negative consequences of multiculturalism. Some nationalists accuse Muslim extremist groups of being a misled section of society and troublemakers.

Moreover, government introduced a citizenship test to ensure that the addition of new colours into the body of British society would increase in its beauty, but the case is different here. The social integration process has failed; plurality, diversity and positivity have all disappeared. Immigrants have brought no positive change to British society as they are less educated, oppressed and belong to the deprived classes of their countries of origin.

The London riots and hate incidents across the country do appear to have crystallized a wider sense of fear in British society. The perceived decline of multiculturalism and 'Britishness', the emergence of armed gangs and private militias and anger at the process of social transformation of the state has increased in the frustration of state authorities. There are more serious law and order issues that could even lead to civil war in near future.

Drug abuse, trafficking, addiction, violent crime, family breakdown, culture of violence, loss of traditional values, behaviour of Borough Councils and their way of unfairly treating tenants, drinking, the culture of boy and girl friend and the failed social education system are considered to be the main causes behind the death of multiculturalism in the country. In Britain, ethnic communities complain that multiculturalism is being imposed on them by the ethnic majority's culture. These and other things have created a strong sense of insecurity in society.

Though British PM warned that a culture of fear would not be allowed on Britain's streets, the law enforcement agencies have so far not been able to professionally tackle the environment of fear. The police acts cautiously due to a fear of community reaction and failed to bring harmony and trust to society due to their deep involvement in fighting the increasing number in crimes and frustration. *"We will do whatever is necessary to restore law and order on our streets."* the PM said in a televised statement. However, the PM accepted that multiculturalism had left some white Britons feeling unfairly treated.

The PM must understand that criminal gangs and extremist organisations still control the streets, educational institutions (*colleges and universities*), departments and financially vulnerable people. They still control the lives of young people. Years ago, Asian and African communities were allotted their own cultural and religious blocs. When they became strong politically and religiously, and through the controlled labour market, they were considered a threat on the pretext that they had started living double lives. These and some other attitudes kept them distanced from white Britons.

They never desired to integrate into British society and never shared their social and cultural values with white Britons. They live according to their own way of life, their children study in their own established schools and madrassas and their business activities are mostly confined to their own communities. Councils and towns have played no specific role in bringing them closer into a state-designed social framework; they never thought about their alienation, deprivation and poverty. Councils never considered the cases of vulnerable people on priority in their housing policies.

There are thousands highly educated men and women in both the Asian and African communities *(educated from the universities of their countries of origin),* but councils, towns, police and other government institutions never tried to use their expertise and experience. They were experts, writers, analysts, journalists, police officers, economists and educationists in their own countries. They could have played an important and constructive role in British society if they had been provided an opportunity by the government and private sector. Consequently, they are living in poverty and frustration.

London's social unrest, looting and burning exposed a broken section of society. Multiculturalism and moral relativism have little to do with the present failed social transformation process. The government of PM Cameron recently reviewed some counter-terrorism and national cohesion strategies amid concern that police and other social organizations are working closely with communities that do not fully recognize liberal values. But this process of changing the level of threat, policies and strategies proved less effective in bringing these communities back on track.

As we understand, multicultural policies of government saved no life in Britain, therefore, a new framework and long-term program is a constant need to tackle the issue of race relations. Some police quarters say multiculturalism has made no specific progress because communities are not interested in mixing their colours into the British society.

They stress the need that all communities are to be encouraged to mix. Research scholars in Britain and Europe are of the opinion that multiculturalism is a dead concept. Britain from the very beginning mishandled the process of immigration. Every illiterate, unskilled and professional criminal was welcomed in order to create a strong consumer market, but it caused many problems.

# CHAPTER 2

## WHY EXTREMISTS AND JIHADISTS HATE BRITAIN?

The recent arrests of some extremist elements across the UK and the prevailing sectarian tendencies have threatened the national security of the country. The story they described before the police investigators about their international links exposed many new things. Some American analysts understand that the United Kingdom is a safe haven of terrorists, extremists, criminal mafia, war lords, war criminals and the world most wanted murderers who have been involved in the killing of innocent people around the world. Among these wanted war criminals, Afghani and Rwandan are the most dagerous people. More than **75** Afghan war criminals are living here and abuse the system.

In an interview with a local newspaper, Home Secretary said, *"I think for too long there's been complacency around universities"*. Comments of Home Secretary came before the government updated counter-terrorism strategy release. Some intelligence reports indicate that terrorist attacks in Britain are likely because threat comes from home-grown terror networks. On 9 November 2010, the Home Secretary announced a review of *PREVENT*, the counter-terrorist programme but terrorism experts criticised the newly updated prevent strategy and viewed it as a failed attempt.

Moreover, the networks of several suspected terror groups and their propaganda campaign across UK is matter of great concern. Somali militant group, al Shabab has established its links here. Algerian Armed Islamic Group, Boko Haram, Taliban, Arab extremist groups, Pakistani and Bangladeshi sectarian groups have established strong terror finance links in towns and cities and channel millions Pound to their respective networks. As the government has kept silence about their illegal activities, analysts in Asia and Africa complain that Britain promotes its foreign policy objectives through the collusion with radical Muslim groups.

The most interesting thing is that Britain police, counter terrorism institutions and every new government is complaining about the prevailing extremist culture in the country on one hand and avoid any violent action against them due to the fear of backlash in the African and Asian communities on the other. In Britain, political analysts understand that today or tomorrow, these terror addicted elements can any time join terrorist organizations in Northern Ireland. As these groups have already established links in the province, they will face no hurdle in joining the violent waves in the province. They have British or EU passports, their families live here and they operate from a safe heaven.

Their presence in various government departments including the police made them capable to influence the decisions making process in cabinet and parliament. Due to their political pressure and disagreement among the cabinet members, a new review of the prevent strategy was delayed in June 2011. Michael Gove and Lord Carlile, in charge the new prevent review argued for crackdown on non-violent Muslim groups, while Deputy Prime Minister said there must be distinction between violent and non-violent extremism. Extremist are more powerful than the expectations of the government. They are intimidating women, homosexuals and Muslims in colleges and universities.

In view of recent sectarian clashes in Northern Ireland and in parts of England, political commentators believe that Britain is losing the battle against extremists and sectarian mafia by relaxing its counter terror policies. Home Secretary, Theresa May became more disturbed by the re-emergence of extremism and sectarianism in Britain. Prime Minister David Cameron once said his country cannot tolerate Islamic extremism, but notwithstanding his harsh stand against these elements, the Prime Minister eat with them on the same table. The government fears lest the fire of ethnic and sectarian violence ignite across the UK. The issue of fake indefinite visas circulation across the country is considered to be a bigger security threat. British Indefinite visa is easily available.

Another interesting story circulating across the country is the presence of 400 war criminals here. Anti-genocide campaigners complain that hundreds of war criminals from across Asia and Africa are living here with "impunity" because the country legal loopholes are the biggest firebrand in prosecuting them. At present, there are more than 400 war criminals living in the UK, suspected of war crimes, torture and genocide. In the Immigration Department, a special war crimes unit recently recommended action against 495 war criminals but government has kept close eyes.

In 4 February 2011, Guardian reported: "*The 383 suspects*

*include 105 from Iraq, 75 from Afghanistan, 73 from Sri Lanka, 39 from Rwanda, 32 from Zimbabwe and 26 from the Democratic Republic of Congo. They are believed to include senior officials from Saddam Hussein's regime, a senior Afghan intelligence service official alleged to be involved in torture and a former police chief from the Democratic Republic of Congo, who confessed in a radio interview to overseeing torture".*

Another same story is being repeated in print and electronic media these days is the issue of sectarian conflict in Northern Ireland and Scotland. The story of Northern Ireland is being complicated by invisible forces, invisible links and networks. Religious sectarianism, fanaticism, extremism, racism and discrimination, altogether are scratching and biting the beautiful and colourful body of the state. Sectarian conflict in Northern Ireland has taken different forms at different times, but has consistently been fuelled by extremism. As the most divided society in the world, sectarian conflict in Northern Ireland is developing into a frightening form.

In 1965, the first race relations law was passed but couldn't prove effective as attacks on different communities continue. Common people fear they may face the consequences of future sectarian conflict in Northern Ireland. The interests of the working class are not fully represented by political parties. One Great Churchill said: "we have nothing to fear, but fear it".

The main cause of violent sectarian movements together is fear. Religious extremists are united by fear whether they are Christian, Muslim, or Jew. Terrorist and extremist groups in the UK will adapt a new technique and have also been quick to use new technologies. They are improving their abilities, way of operations and attacks. In future, Britain will face more violence, more terror attacks and more sectarian clashes in Northern Ireland.

## Britain's police, multiculturalism and racism

Multiculturalism in Britain failed and saved no lives. The government institutions are weeping and frustrated on the virus penetrated into their rank and file. Those involved in terror-related incidents and the recent riots in the country came from different cultures, races and religions. The recent riots and economic terrorism on the streets of Britain and the way it was tackled raised many question about the performance and credibility of the police and its intelligence units.

During violence and disorder, Britain's police officers encountered trouble and failed to protect public and government properties across the country. Though factors behind these riots were numerous, the most concerning developments in the UK's political and social fields have been the emergence of racism, discrimination, Islam-phobia and the prevailing criminal culture of recent years. The issues of burning the holy Quran, derogatory cartoons of Prophet Muhammad (PBUH), religious dress, the Burqa, the issue of Halal and Haraam food shops and the acts of terrorism by some Muslim extremist groups in and outside the UK, have all created plenty of misunderstandings among the followers of different faiths.

Another development that has taken place just recently is the troubled relationship between cultural diversity. No doubt, there has been progress on race relations in the past but racism continues to blight many lives. There is a lack of the optimistic concept of integrated society in the country. The threat to national security not only emanates from Scottish, Welsh and Irish nationalism, multiculturalism has pitted communities against each other.

In the absence of a sophisticated and political response to cultural diversity and plurality, many white and black issues remained untouched. Blacks and Asians complain they are not treated equally, while whites say their country's citizenship has been contaminated. Mark Perryman (2009) views the issue from a different perspective:

*"Debates about Welsh, Scottish, Irish or English identity were conducted in isolation from the multicultural question. Britain's broad pattern of allegiance within, across and between, was lost in the homogenising tendency of nation building . . . however, it is clear a new discourse of multiculturalism is required."*

Though the doctrine of multiculturalism inculcates in us that communities should not be forced to integrate, recently this idea has come under attack while minorities are going into isolation. In Yasmin Alibhai-Brown's (*Daily Telegraph, May 23, 2000*) understanding, black people are now retreating into tribal identities instead of thinking of themselves. They demand attention and resources for their particular patch. In her well-researched article, Brown has revealed that:

*"The English are understandably disgruntled that their ethnicity is denied while all other identities—Welsh, Scottish, Hindu, Caribbean and the rest—are celebrated."*

The issue of racism in the police department has badly

affected the professional abilities of the force. Last year, the Equality and Human Rights Commission in its report concluded that the metropolitan police was responsible for 120,000 'excessive' stop-and-search incidents against people from ethnic minorities in 2008 and 2009. On August 25, 2011, the Daily Mail reported an independent inquiry into the aspects of alleged racism in the metropolitan police department.

On February 5, 2011, Prime Minister David Cameron accepted his country's failure to maintain long term policy of multiculturalism. He complained that this policy is responsible for fostering Islamic extremism. "Under the doctrine of state multiculturalism, we have encouraged different cultures to live separate lives, a part from each other and a part from the mainstream. We have failed to provide a vision of society to which they feel they want to belong. We have even tolerated these segregated communities behaving in way that run completely counter to our values. "He said.

Many observers in Europe support Mr. Cameron views but say it is too late now to complain. The current model of multiculturalism has failed as Britishness disappeared and races hate each other in streets and in their business communities. Recently Deputy Prime Minister Nick Clegg accused banks for racism. Nick Clegg argued British banks to keep balance but complained that banks holding black people back from the last frontier of racial economic equality. According to the Guardian report; "The reputation of British banks will take a fresh battering when the deputy Prime Minister accused then of discrimination against members of ethnic minorities in the way they distribute loans and set interest rates."

Social scientists have warned that a new society of violent sectarian element and professional criminals is being promoted by underground mafia groups in the United Kingdom. The culture of violence is prevailing and the values of British society are badly abused by these groups. Drug trafficking culture of Asian communities, knife culture of black criminals and extremist tendencies have created the environment of fear and harassment.

Sir Bill Morris was requested to carry out an investigation into the racist behaviour of the officers. The investigation found cases, specifically, of Superintendent Ali Dizai and Officer Sergeant Gurpal Singh Virdi who were sacked after being falsely accused of sending hate mail. On April 29, 2011, the Daily Mail reported that a lady police constable, Hinah Parekh, had resigned over racist abuse and bullying in the Metropolitan Police. Hinah Parekh said racist abuse from fellow police officers caused her to suffer from depression and stress.

Reform processes in the police department and cleaning up the institution of unionists and political interference is another challenge. According to a former UK police chief, politics in the police need to be investigated. A number of attempts to modernise the police, their integrated technology, skills, training and re-balancing the criminal justice system were made in the past, but positive changes in the police method of fighting criminal gangs never occurred.

The Home Affairs Select Committee recently completed some inquiries into policing in the UK and focused on what is likely to be the key element of reforms. The committee finally published a comprehensive police and crime commissioner's report in December 2010. In the recent riots, the cold war between the police and government authorities in various cities remained irksome.

The Home Secretary criticised the police chiefs for their handling of the violence while police officers rejected the prime minister's decision to hire a former New York and LA police chief as an adviser in the wake of the riots. Another issue that widened the clefts between the police and government was the row over police funding and the need to surge so many officers onto the streets. The police clearly feel aggrieved that they have been criticised for the way they handled the riots.

Though the home office, in its recent report, 'Equality, Diversity and Human Rights Strategy for the Police Service', has claimed that policing has undergone a transformation over recent years and it has positively responded to the changes in society, the recent riots proved that the police and its intelligence units are still not able to tackle any major unrest across the country.

The home office, association of chief police officers and association of police authorities with the support of the National Policing Improvement Agency (NPIA) are responsible for closely monitoring racism and discrimination in the police department. But how they are monitoring it is the question. There is no change in police behaviour when it comes to treating people in the police stations and streets.

If the home office and NPIA report on equality and diversity of the police and their monitoring policy in response to a number of reviews of the Bradley Report (2009), the

Independent Police Complaints Authority Report (2008), the Commission for Racial Equality's (CRE) Formal Investigation into the Police Service (2003) and the Stephen Lawrence Enquiry Report (1999), during the last 10 years, is fully implemented then we can expect there will be an improvement in the performance of the UK police. The issue of extremism needs to be gradually resolved because Western policies in Iraq and Afghanistan gifted extremism to young Muslims in Britain. Muslim scholars have warned that the new war front in Libya may further widen gap between Muslim and Christians.

# CHAPTER 3

## RADICALIZATION AND THE THREAT OF EXTREMISM

In all chapters of my book, I have highlighted the threat of extremism and radicalization in the United Kingdom. Britain based Muslim extremists have gained financial power by collecting a lot of money from different communities and opened secret recruiting centres. These groups have sent hundreds of their young members to Somalia, Nigeria, Sudan, Pakistan, Iraq, Yemen, Libya and Afghanistan for fight against their governments. They defeated Qaddafi, fighting Assad and tomorrow they will join the terrorist Taliban network in Middle East and Persian Gulf region.

These extremist networks prevent people from integration into British society. Prime Minister David Cameron has already complained about the failure of his country long-standing policy of multiculturalism. Mr. Cameron understands that the policies of previous government caused the problem, but mix reaction was shown on his statement. European Union welcomed his statement while Britain based extremists repudiated him and said Muslim have there own way of life and culture. As Vikileak reported: *"UK passport holders will be recruited to commit terrorist operations."* Another document revealed that Britain based extremist groups are a constant threat to security.

On December 12, 2009, a UK Africa Regional Counter-terrorism Conference was told that British Muslims are travelling to Somalia for jihad and more than 1000 British passport holder live in a largest religious school (Hargeisa) in Somaliland region. The British failed policies on extremism compelled the United States to launch an independent campaign against the UK based extremist groups.

Britain has the biggest collection of Somali extremists as government in London recently revealed about seventy British Somali nationals were believed to be travelling to Somalia for terror training every year. Law and order in the UK is deteriorating day by day and the looming terror threat is intensified. On February 4, 2010, Daily Independent reported that army may start patrolling streets due to confront terror threat:

*"Britain's armed forces could be used on a regular basis on the streets of Britain to confront the threat of terrorism, under the terms of a strategic defence review announced yesterday, the newspaper reported".*

Keeping in view the growing terror threat of international terrorism and domestic extremism, Britain intelligence agencies fight in this battlefield and adopted three distinct roles. It produces strategic assessment; act as a global policeman by monitoring terror networks and helping other states in fighting terrorism. A well organized intelligence agency, SIS tackles global terror networks. As we mentioned earlier, sectarian violence in both Scotland and Northern

Ireland, can anytime create security problems. In England level, efforts are under way for tackling this menace effectively, but in Scotland, the issue has become more sensitive.

To tackle the threat of present and future sectarian violence in Scotland, the government established Scottish Preventing Extremism Unit (SPVEU) with the association of Chief Police Officers Scotland, in 2009. Scotland has a bitter experience of sectarian violence of the past. In our chapters, we warned about the international espionage threat, as several states are actively seeking advance information in Britain institutions. In Britain, presently, intelligence agencies are tracking two thousands suspected people for their links with terror groups and, investigations over two hundred networks.

Terror attacks in Moscow underground station was, in fact, a message of al Qaeda terror network to the Russian authorities that it can target any place in the country. Al Qaeda carried out successful attacks in London, Spain, Pakistan, Afghanistan and parts of Africa in the past. In Moscow, two female suicide bombers killed at least 40 people and 70 injured. The Lubyanka station is located next to the Russian Federal Security Service Headquarters, and is also near the Kremlin. According to sources, Muslim extremists of Caucasus region want to establish their own state. During the last two decade of war with Russia, over 500,000 people left Chechnya.

Not only Somalia is the source of extremism and militancy in Britain, Pakistan, Afghanistan and Bangladesh are more serious security threat to the country. As we mentioned earlier, a suicide bomber from Ealing Broadway, London, had blown himself up in an attack in Somalia that killed more than twenty soldiers. Two Somali asylum-seekers were among the four men convicted of the failed attempts to bomb the London transport system on 21 July 2005. Moreover, a conservative British member parliament, Chairman Counter Terrorism Subcommittee once said:

*"I have seen figures that are not in the public domain that suggest there is an increasing flow of young Britons into Somalia. There is now a mixture of British people, from numerous backgrounds, who are heading out there and that are causing great concern."* In my previous papers, I had warned about the growing number of suspect visits to Somalia. British Somali who want to visit Somalia cross the border from Kenya.

Sheikh Ahmed, a Somali religious leader in London, once said that he had heard from families of sons travelling to Somalia to join Islamist groups. According to terror monitor report, American Somali are actively participating in jihad in Somalia. There are numerous instances of European Muslims joining al-Shabab and the ICU. The great concern is not what these people do while in Somalia but what happens when they return to the countries from which they came. It is a concern not only for the US but Britain as well.

The challenge posed by jihadi networks to the UK security is matter of great concern. These networks are deeply involved in drug trafficking across the country, run religious schools and recruit young students. According to the MI5 previous calculations more than 200 extremist networks operate in the country. From jails to madrassa, thousands extremists are promoting the process of radicalization.

The issue of racism and sectarianism in the United

Kingdom, specifically, in Northern Ireland, has become a big problem for the security agencies and the police. As BBC reported: *"more than one hundred families left their homes in Belfast due to the fear of racist attacks."* The presence of Indian, Chinese and other Asian communities and their religious affiliation can be seen as matter of concern. During the ceasefire period, thousands residents came back to their towns but some racist elements further created more problems in the region.

On July 2, 2009, in Belfast, attacks were carried out against the Romanian communities. Home grown extremism here has become a bigger problem as the rising trends of radicalization signified that the threat of terrorism is no longer come from international terror networks, self radicalized groups and self organized home grown extremist networks pose a growing threat to British society.

Those who became radicalized are educated and active in their communities. Some might come from deprived families, some from poor and some from sectarian families who generally follow the principles of hate culture. Some experts understand that radicalization starts with individuals who are frustrated, poor, unemployed, oppressed and dejected of their society or domestic foreign policy of their governments.

The threat from international terrorism and home grown jihadi extremist forces is already existed. Northern Ireland related terror threat is shaping into a new danger. Terrorist and sectarian elements along with their foreign partners are looking for various means to create a war like situation in the province. International extremist and terrorist groups are trying to penetrate into the region. Racism, discrimination and sectarianism, extremism and takfiri jihadism are issues, which can create a bigger national security threat in near future.

Though government and state institutions have deeply concentrated on international terrorism, Afghanistan and other areas of interest, but internal security and concordance need an intellectual approach. On 25 May 2011, Home Affairs Committee launched an enquiry to find out how the roots of radicalization were established. The committee decided to find risk factors for recruitment to terror groups, the basic roots of prisons criminal networks and to make recommendations to inform implementation of the government's prevent strategy. The committee completed it work and made recommendations but we all understand that religious and sectarian ideologies are the driving force behind the process of radicalization.

Sectarian mafia networks are trying day and night to indoctrinate and radicalize young people and use them against other sects. Experts of social science understand that students belong to middle-class provide the most fertile ground for the implementation of the strategies of these sectarian and extremist groups. Terrorist who carried out the London and Madrid suicide attacks were from middle class society?

Daily Telegraph, on Nov 11, 2008, quoted the government leaked report saying, thousands extremists and takfiri jihadists live in Britain with their violent jihadi culture. According to the report: *"For the foreseeable future the UK will continue to be a high-priority target for international terrorists aligned with al Qaeda"*. It will face a threat from British nationals, including Muslim converts, and UK-based foreign terrorists, as well as terrorists planning attacks from abroad. Extremist networks are principally engaged in spreading their extremist message, training, fund raising and procuring non-lethal military equipment to support the jihads in Pakistan, Afghanistan and Iraq, and sending recruits to the conflicts."

Al Qaeda terror network has extensive training facilities across Europe. Extremist and terrorist groups recruiting young generation in European states. About the Al Shabab, what I had predicted proved to be true. Other jihadist groups in Somalia, such as Hizbul Islam. Al Shabab publicly pledged allegiance to Osama bin Laden in September 2009 and therefore has formally joined the ranks of al Qaeda's regional franchise groups. Afghanistan, Pakistan, Somalia, Yemen, Iran, Iraq, Palestine and Saudi Arabia still remain a threat, to be kept under watch permanently.

In future, these groups in Europe and the United Kingdom can disrupt the security network anytime. The Internet, that most contemporary of media, is increasingly its medium of choice: Jihadist websites, forums and blogs flourish. They have trained cyber warriors and information warfare experts to easily destroy the institutional networks of major European countries.

The networks of takfiri jihadists and the interplay between these networks, social and political elements, have empowered radical groups whose spread in the UK caused national security threats. The international dimension of these groups is being promoted by British born radicalized immigrants of Afghani, Pakistan, Bangladeshi, Somali, Sudanese and the Arabs origin to introduce the country as a hub of radicalization and extremism. These UK based groups openly invite young people to their propaganda networks. They train them and use them in their terror related activities.

# CHAPTER 4

## HOW POLICE LOST THE TRUST OF COMMUNITIES?

In the police laws, every person is constable, whatever its actual rank is, it means officers and constable have equal powers of arrest. The police have the authority to keep a person for twenty four hours in the police station. According to the Police Act 1996, section 30: *"a member of a police force shall have all the powers and privileges of a Constable throughout England and Wales and the adjacent United Kingdom waters"*. The Scotland Yard Police Act of 1967 specify the jurisdiction of the police, the force is responsible to the Secretary of State.

On the immigration field, UK Border Agency is an active police force. The function of the force has been divided into five unified operations: border, international, immigration, intelligence and detention. Each operation is conducted by a director. According to the police websites and reports, reforms in the police department are needed. Scotland Yard, experts say, is the institution capable in tackling organized crime.

The police force became more important since the Metropolitan Police Act of 1829 was passed by Home Secretary Sir Robert Peel, but the recent wave of crime and one million illegal immigrants entered the country created a precarious situation for the police. With the implementation of this act, the police force came into existence. Due to the developing situation in and outside the country, in 1890, the Metropolitan Police number increased from 1,000 to 13,000 forces. In 1907 and 1940, New Scotland Yard was extended further.

New Scotland Yard established the CID department in 1878. The most important intelligence agency (Special Irish Branch) was formed in 1883. The Criminal Investigation Department (CID), established in April 1878, has a brilliant history of tackling crime and criminal cultures in various Asian and African countries. This department now tackles crime and carries out investigation into criminal cases, across the United Kingdom. In all police stations, detective officers are inducted. All these officers are responsible to the detective chief inspector.

As for as the police role in law and order is concerned, we discussed the deteriorating law and order situation in the United Kingdom in previous pages, now we will estimate the police force combating the prevailing criminal culture across the country. There are different types of police forces and private security agencies in the UK. Majority work of the policing is being carried out by the territorial police force. The police acts 1996, 1967 and 2000, highlight the jurisdiction and responsibilities of the police.

At present, more than one hundred forty five thousands police force is in full operation in the country, in partnership with more than hundred private security agencies and intelligence networks. Notwithstanding, UK Border Agency, New Scotland Yard Police, Her Majesty's

Inspectorate of Constabulary, Criminal Investigation Department, Metropolitan Police, Diplomatic Protection Group, National Crime Force and Home Office law and order strategies, no specific improvement in law and order in the country is seen. Criminal gangs are getting strong day by day, and the network of criminal market economy is expanded.

Due to some terror networks, police in the country used to prepare and develop a comprehensive counter terrorism strategy. This strategy was developed in partnership with various intelligence agencies. The Police Superintendents Association in 2004 submitted proposals to the Home Secretary, which envisaged a three-tier system based on two hundred seventy local police divisions and ten regional controllers, with regional police units for public order and major investigations, and presumably the national units and agencies like Serious Organized Crime Agency.

The Home Office function has been confined to countering terrorism by the Prime Minister in 2007. According to the Prime Minister announcement, the Home Office tackles immigration and policing as well. Police experts in the country have recently designed comprehensive strategy, intercepting Muslim communities, becoming violent extremists.

The Association of Police Officers believes this strategy will help schools in intercepting radical ideas of extremist groups. After the London bombing in 2005 and 2007, consultations started related to the future response to terrorism across the country. The Home Office figures, showing the breakdown by ethnic origin category, show that from 2001–2004; those stopped and arrested under anti terror laws of 2000 were, majority Asian.

The most important issue in the domestic management of terrorism in the country is the location that clearly shows the wide geographical spread of arrests. A Home Office report issued in Nov 26, 2009, discusses the police power under the terrorism act 2000, and gives details of stops and search outcomes in 2008 and 2009. The London Home Office had published this type of a comprehensive report in May 2009 and the recently released report is the latest and update.

This report, according to the Home Office sources, has full details of present law and order situation in the country. This report brings together, complete statistical materials from police and other agencies. As per the recently published report (Nov 2009), in 2008/9, the police arrested some one hundred ninety terror suspects, compared with two hundred thirty one in 2007. The police in the UK have arrested 1,661 terror suspects from across the country since 2001. Among the 190 terror suspects arrested in 2009, 123 were arrested under section 41 of the terror laws 2000.

Charges for terror arrest, the report notes, are not limited to offences under terror legislation; many offences are dealt with under other legislation, e.g. conspiracy to murder, are not covered in terrorism legislation. The 2000 Act of terrorism in the United Kingdom provides with the police force an opportunity to exercise the power of search and stop. According to the report details, under this law, some 256,026 people were stopped and arrested in 2008 and 2009. This action of the police, as we have already mentioned earlier, created more distance between the police and community. Under section 43 of the terrorism act 2000, according to the Home Office recent report for 2000:

*"The Terrorism Act also gives powers for individual officers to stop and search a suspect whom he/she reasonably suspects of being involved in terrorism activity. Information collected from the Metropolitan Police Service shows that in 2008/9 1,643 persons were stopped and searched under these powers."*

The police stop and search program has created more trouble for Asian and European citizens. People complain against the behaviour of the police in trains, buses and on roads. Some were humiliated, searched inhumanly and asked irrelevant questions. In 2009, Guardian newspaper in its editorial reported:

*"The claim that policing has become dangerously over centralized is now a political commonplace. But it is not just a slogan. Good policing depends on local support, on the willingness of individual citizens to come forward as witness or to support dubious activity."*

The police authority needs to gain its mandate by consulting local people effectively about policing issues, seeking their views on matters such as the level of the policing precept, divisional and force policing plans and their experience of day-to-day policing. In Britain, there are innumerable police forces, agencies and private security agencies, which play very important role in safeguarding the state and its institutions. In spite all these forces and their struggle in tackling violent crimes and extremism in the country, criminal gang's networks are in full operation.

The Secretive Police Force in the UK has been enrolled and

promoted by the Association of Chief Police Officers (ACPO) is, at present, in the field and mostly tackling extremism in the United Kingdom. Another unit of the police is National Extremism Tactical Coordination Unit (NETCO) that working under the command of the ACPO.

People working in the NETCO and WECTU have been inducted from the police department. The basic job of these forces is policing, everyone knows about the basic philosophy and function of both these police forces. NETCO, experts believe is a private body, but receive financial support from the government. As mentioned earlier, police with all resources, has not been able to tackle the prevailing criminal culture effectively.

It needs the cooperation of the private security agencies. The police have fed up from tackling the prevailing criminal gang culture. Therefore, it needs the cooperation of the Private security agencies that play important role in maintaining law and order. However, Unregulated and poor management of these security agencies, expert say, can create more trouble for the good governance. Generally, private security agencies provide security to the people and help the police in eradicating crime.

Newspapers in the UK published interesting stories about these security agencies. According to the Guardian these agencies tackle terror incidents even in educational institutions. In October 2006, Special Branch that worked closely with MI5 in the past was merged with anti terrorism branch and restructured to form a new command of counter terrorism in the country. To make more effective the war on domestic terrorism and extremism, another security unit, titles National Public Order Intelligence Unit (NPOIU) was set up by ACPO in 1999.

In February 2009, newspapers reported ACPO changing the role of NPOIU and extending its mandate on tackling domestic extremist threat in the country. According to the Daily Mail report, the confidential intelligence can operate across the country because within the NPOIU, a new unit of intelligence was set up. At present, multinational corporations and private sector are the strategic partners of the government. Security experts say, for the police training, protection of important installations, the destruction of ammunition stockpiles and the removal of small arms, private sector companies are hired.

However, it means the nature of security environment has changed ultimately. According to the DEMOs research paper, at home, the responsibility of private sector regarding national security has grown since privatization began in 1980s. As we are living in the twenty first century, this century offers a radically different political landscape for debating national security. Security experts say government and the police have come under an ultimate influence of multinational security agencies.

The recent debates on trust deficit between the UK police and communities, the police way of conducting some recent operations, racism, discrimination and search and stop under the Counter Terrorism Act 2000, raised many questions. Communities complain about the inactive presence and invisible participation of police in streets and towns and demand that delivering policing—whether in form of force or service should not be based on discrimination.

The day to day increasing distrust between communities and the police are matter of great concern not only for the government in power but for the Home Office and policing improvement agency as well. A new image of the London police appeared after the recent riots is considered to be contradictory as the police demonstrated inconsiderably. This is not the first time riots hit Britain society, there were race riots in South Shields, Glasgow, London's East End, Liverpool, Cardiff, Barry, and Newport. In 1930, immigrants started protests in East London during the 1930s and Notting Hill in the 1950s. In 1980, in the area of Black minority communities, racism, discrimination and poverty sparked a series of riots.

In 1981, 1982 and 1985, there have been riots in various cities. In 2004, more than 87,000 minority residents told British they had been a victim of a racially motivated crime. The Race Relations Act 1965 outlawed public discrimination. Further Acts in 1968 and 1976 outlawed discrimination in employment. In 2001, there were racial riots in both Bradford and Oldham and in 2005; riots in Birmingham and Brixton were against the police behaviour. In 2008, an organization (London Children Bureau) released a 366 pages report in which they recognized racist behaviour in young children. Hassan Ali in his article, (November 2003) has presented a racist image of Britain police in these words:

*"Top police and the government have been at pains to argue that racism in the police is merely a reflection of wider society. This is nonsense. It is clear from the programme that the 'canteen culture' of bigotry in the police is at a level way above most of British society—only matched by that in other authoritarian jobs such as the armed services and prison officers."*

Among all Asian and Africans ethnic groups, majority of their members have reservation about the police behaviour and not willing to report even a single crime to the police as they understand that police has shown no specific interest in resolving their issues in the past. They are now thinking on the line that police is only for the white people. For example, they complain that in many occasions the police favoured whites instead of tackling an incident impartially. Home Office is trying to establish the fact that citizens' involvement in policing has become a central element in its reform agenda, but the story here is different.

Citizens and the police department are thinking adversely. A report in 2010 found that fifty percent of Muslims across the UK believe that racism has spread to all sections of society in the past several years. Pakistani, Indian, Afghani, Bangladeshi, Somali, Sudanese and other black and white colours feel they are loyal British citizens but police treat them in a racial way. They complain that police often targets ethnic minorities with a specific behaviour which later on causes a lot of misunderstanding between communities and the police.

The above mentioned misunderstanding and trust deficit between the police and community are considered to be a bigger challenge not only for Home Office, Policing Improvement Agency but for the National City Community and Police Relations Commission as well. These trust deficits cannot be understood unless the constraints on both sides are thoroughly explored.

Researcher Marshall Carter supports my perception of police-community relations in these words: *"What the police and community think and feel about each other reflect their own past experience and the images transmitted through friends, education, the media and popular stereotypes".* One another aspect of citizens complaints is that police has often responds to unrests in a non-professional way which is not acceptable in any way.

In response to all complaints of minority communities, police complains that minority groups never thought to mix their colours within British society and regret that multiculturalism has made no specific progress. They stress the need that all communities are to be encouraged to mix. Institute of Applied Social Studies in Birmingham University recently completed a research paper which suggests the establishment of good relationships between the police and local community members, and stresses the need on police information sharing with community.

The issue of policing and police community relations in Britain is very complicated. Some recent news stories of police involvement in corruption cases, phone hacking, its contradictory role after the London riots and racism further transmogrified its image. The police criminal justice system is under fire due to the increasing number of prison population, unrest within the Prison System and deaths in custody. There are different police authorities in Britain and each one is comprised of 17 members, nine councillors, three magistrates and five independent, but this is not clear how much they are effective in maintaining law and order.

The police Act of 1964 gives the police more powers, Crime and Disorder Act of 1998 deals with crime and disorder, local government Act of 1999 order the police to achieve best value in delivering policing in communities, the Race Relations Act (2000) is related to race equality and public access to policing information, but in spite of all these legal restrictions, instructions and responsibilities, no specific improvement occurred in the police way of tackling community problems and maintaining law and order management.

Police administration has never been able to closely observe diversity, colours and their ethnic relations. But Metropolitan Police Service deny these allegations and says that it is committed on working collaboratively with communities, boroughs and partners to identify effective solutions to serious crime problems.

The increasing power of criminal mafia groups, the deep rooted black market economy, the presence of 400 hundred war criminals of different ethnicities, unemployment, poverty, the prevailing criminal culture in society, the failure of multiculturalism, racism and trust deficit between the police and community are considered to be greater challenges for the British police administration. Population terrorism and the invasion of illiterate armies from Asian and European continents has irritated Home Secretary Theresa May that how can her administration tackle this irregular invasion. She is considering professional way to tackled this and other law and order issues.

Home Secretary now stressed the need on police reforms which is clearly indicative of her inner pain regarding the police failure in restoring the confidence of business community. Home Office, police and research institutions have carried out innumerable surveys to find out professional ways for bringing about social concordance and harmony to British society, but all these efforts proved less fruitful. The recent consultation paper (*Policing in the 21st Century: Recon-*

*necting police and people*) proposed the introduction of elected police and crime commissioners. This proposal was supported by the government.

In response to the proposal, government promised to elect individuals who will over see the check and balance system. Policing and Criminal Justice Minister, Nick Herbert has recently launched a public consultation campaign on the future of police leadership. Speaking about the new consultation he said; *"In challenging times we need strong and focused leadership in the police."*

# CHAPTER 5

## RACISM AND THE POLICE DEPARTMENT

The disease of racism has penetrated into all state institutions in the United Kingdom. Institutional racism in the police department has badly affected its basic abilities, professionalism and function. The issue of black, white and Asian unionism is much complicated which is a biggest obstruction that disrupts the coordination process. In many occasion, white police officers were found sending text messages of derogatory remarks to their Asian and black colleagues.

Consequently, in 2003, some racist police officers from Manchester, Wales, and other department were forced to resign due to their racist behaviour. In March 4, 2008, BBC reported twelve more racist police officers were punished. The Police Reform Act 2002 was introduced with the aim of increasing public confidence in the police complaints system and, ultimately, the police service as a whole. The Act introduced a series of fundamental changes to the existing police complaints system but no change occurred in the police attitude towards communities. The reform laws and accountability bills are just in paper, in reality, police follow century old way of policing.

As we have already discussed the issue of racism in Northern Ireland and Scotland, violence has now spread across the country as white, black and Asian student attack each other in schools and colleges. In 2009 alone, over 40,000 thousands incidents of racism were reported in schools across the country. Daily Telegraph in its report revealed these incidents in Britain schools. The issue is much complicated while the police have failed to control these incidents.

From 2002–2006, over ninety five thousands racist incidents were reported in schools and colleges across the country. The government then introduced CD music in which tolerance has been requested. As per the newspapers reports, the UK police have badly failed in tackling racism threat in the country. On October 19, 2008, three Asian police officers filed racism charges against the London Metropolitan Police. On April 2, 2004, the Independent reported the complaint of a black women police officer in Manchester.

Chief Inspector Police Karin Mulligan complained about her sexual harassment and racist behaviour. Muslim communities in Britain often complain against the police racist behaviour. The Muslim News criticized the government and agencies for using Muslim women as informer in its misguided campaign against radicalization as opposed to addressing the problems they face through discrimination such as high rates of unemployment. The police now must change their behaviours and focus its efforts on tackling these issues within its own workforce. According to the report of Internet Journal of Criminology (Black and Asian police officers and support staff: Prejudices, Identity, Agency and Social Cohesion, 2006):

*"One of the main motivation of the British government's*

*movement away from the multiculturalists agenda is that it is now seen as too simplistic and to have contributed to too many inward looking and, therefore, economically disadvantaged communities. These communities are said in popular and political discourse, particularly, post New York's 9/11 and London's 7/7 terrorist attacks, to have advertently contributed towards an ending environment for violent extremism and social unrest."*

There are complaints that Police officers arrest those belong to minority communities at a disproportionate level, even more so if they are black or Asian. Ethnic minority officer's experience is of frequent prejudices and discrimination, expressed through joking, banter and exclusion from full membership of their work team. Editor of the Muslim News Ahmad complained:

*"It is important to empower women to play a greater role in the public life, regardless of their religious persuasion, but the Government seems only intent in focusing on Muslim women to tackle extremism,"* Ahmed said.

Muslims across the United Kingdom have already complained against the anti terror laws of 2000, specifically against the search and stop process. A leader of Muslim Community, Mr. Ahmad warned that the government appeared to have not learnt from the past. In the past, Ahmad claimed the government received no support from the Muslim communities.

There are complaints against the police everywhere in the country. In Plymouth, a Muslim complained against the local police for ignoring his call for help against racist attacks. Abul Azad was threatened and attacked by racists. The section seventy one of the Race Relations Act 2000

(Amended), stresses the need that all institutions require to adopt a policy of the elimination of racism, promote equality and promote race relations. As per the police behaviours, the London mayor once ordered an enquiry into the racism crime of the Metropolitan Police.

The enquiry was ordered while the police association of the black people called upon Asian and blacks, not to join police force. A Muslim Police Commissioner in London, Mr. Ghafoor has been the victim of racism. Tariq Ghafoor filed a case with the employment tribunal levelling charges of racism and discrimination. However, one another Muslim police officer filed his case against the police racist behaviour. IANS reported three senior Asian police officers complaints against the London police department. A Muslim woman, Yasmin Rehman is another victim of racism in the police department.

On October 27, 2008, ANI reported a black intelligence officer was racially assaulted by two white men. He complained that his boss mistreated him racially. Moreover, Daily Telegraph reported Sergeant Gareth, humiliation by his manager that he belonged to the Black Police Association. Another Pakistani origin police cop registered his complaint against a white police officer, saying, that he abused him and laughed on his beard. His white colleague told him that he is superior to him because he was white. Iqbal told the press, notwithstanding his humiliation, he was sacked by the Bedfordshire police administration.

In May 2009, West Yorkshire Police started an enquiry into the involvement of white police officers in the racism cases. This wave of racism, the Sunday Telegraph reported, could impact on West Yorkshire Police ability in tackling extremism in the country. In one case, an ethnic minority officer claimed, he was called a "terrorist" by a senior officer because he was carrying a rucksack. Moreover, five police officers resigned and three were suspended while the BBC documentary reported racism in the police department.

In 1990s, the government introduced Intelligence-Led Policing Programme in the country. The programme has so far been failed due to the day to day increasing criminal incidents and racist attacks. The violent activities of criminal gangs, racist incident and sectarian hatred are the clear example of the police and NIM failure, in tackling the prevailing criminal culture across the country. It must be born in mind, for a safer environment and business climate; credit goes to former Prime Minister Margaret Thatcher, who had tackled the law and order effectively.

In 2000, perceptions changed regarding the investigation and crime control. In the same year National Criminal Intelligence Service with the help of Association of Chief Police Officers piloted National Intelligence Model Agency, an effective law enforcement agency for managing crime, criminals, and local disorder and community issues.

The first National Policing Plan of the British government covered the period from 2003–2006, required all the 43 police forces to adopt National Intelligence Model. NIM ultimately changed the police face. Due to the lake of the police and intelligence concordance on the issue of crime prevention, in 2004, the Cardiff University presented another picture of the police in the country. Some experts believe that for the performance ability of the police, public approval is a must. Cooperation among the communities, police and intelligence agencies on the issue of law enforcement cannot be ignored.

Police need public favour but here in the UK, there are wide-ranging differences between the public and the police. The policing community aspect is weak, police is not able to convince people and not able to win the mind and heart of the local population. This is the basic weakness on the part of police. The Strategic Tasking and Coordination Group, in its all bi-annual meeting advise the police for intelligence collection, but, there are number of intelligence agencies in the UK, devoted to different aspects of intelligence.

We do not blame these agencies have failed in tackling law and order across the country, we just suggest, and that there must be the process of reform in the intelligence community. We understand sometime intelligence failures frequently lead to call for reforms. As we mentioned earlier, ruction over the issue of law and order between the police and agencies, further complicated as the official report revealed that police and agencies are not willing to share information on crime and racism.

The lake of trust, Guardian reported (Nov 8, 2008) among the law enforcement agencies created more problems in the struggle against extremism and violent crime, across the country. The police lake of understanding the day to day worsening law and order situation and racism, within the force are the main issues to be considered seriously. According to the Guardian report: "The Association of Chief Police Officers issued guidance to police forces to encourage them to share critical sensitive information to allow local councils and police commanders to develop more sharply targeted interventions."

Having supported the police force, the British National Party in its statement claimed that: "Although the empirical evidence is overwhelming that knife crime and terrorism in modern Britain originate amongst the black and Muslim communities, the police are still branded as 'racist' when they try and take preventative measures against these crimes. The usual cries of 'institutional racism' have once again been heard with the news that black people are almost eight times as likely as whites to be stopped and searched.

The use of ordinary stop and search tactics in England and Wales raised sharply to more than one million in 2007–08, the highest figure since 1998. The rise has had a disproportionate impact on non-whites." On March 13, 2005, Sunday Times reported a Middle Eastern lawyer threatened the UK police of legal action, for their racist behaviour, with the Arab communities in the country.

The lawyer filed an official complain over the lake of police action, when crime is reported to the police. The claim was prepared by Dead and Dear Solicitors, whose clients included the Saudi Royal Family, the king of Morocco, David Khalili, the wealthy Iranian art dealer and NadhmiAuchi, the newspaper reported. In 2008/09, over four hundred investigations were carried out, which were either independently investigated by the IPCC or had IPCC oversight.

The same year, the IPCC received 4,634 appeals, and members of the public chose to make 14,870 complaints via the IPCC, rather than raising them directly with the police force concerned. In December 2008, Root and Branch Reforms were introduced to the existing systems, for dealing with misconduct, poor performance and poor attendance within the police service. These reforms were introduced, to make the police force more effective across the country.

The culture of institutional concordance, police-community connections and social harmony has been in trouble since the London bombings in 2005 and 2007. Police intelligence agencies are too weak as they do not know about the thousands of illegal immigrants living across the country for the past five to 15 years. The police lost the trust of the community, which started distancing itself from the community policing process.

Community leaders believe that Britain's police is just running about here and there, making noises to show that they are actively pursuing criminal elements while, in reality, they have failed to provide good services to the community. The police have collectively failed in countering multicultural crimes in cities and towns. They need to respect color, culture and different ways of life.

The police and its intelligence have so far badly failed in bringing these people onto their records. The UK Border Agency arrests illegal people and deports them to their countries but, within a month, they come back. There is also no clear strategy for tackling criminal mafia groups. The home office claims that policing has undergone a transformation over recent years and that it has responded to social changes and rising public expectations but communities have complaints against the police's behavior and its way of tackling suspects through counter-terror laws.

How can we accept that the police service has made significant progress when it failed in tackling the recent riots in

London in which they demonstrated a less than professional approach? Another irony is that the police do not properly respond to the complaints of communities and keep them in long lines during the complaints registration process. On many occasions, they do not reach the crime scene on time. Social and administrative connections between the police and communities are weak and based on misunderstandings. We all remember the statements of politicians and public leaders pinpointing the flawed crime strategies of the UK police over the last five years.

On a council level, these and other issues are being tackled through various organizations while their results have always been contradictory. Funds are released to the NGOs, community groups and religious clerics for bringing about concordance and harmony to society but, in spite of all these efforts, a criminal culture prevails, intolerance is on the increase and racism has targeted several government and private institutions, including the police. This wrongly understood way of maintaining law and order and community trust, undoubtedly, has left adverse effects on society.

The Serious Organized Crime Agency (SOCA) has now tired of tackling the corruption cases of the police department day and night. According to a Guardian report, information on police corruption cases is always kept secret. Recent telephone espionage and hacking cases have created more skepticism about the credibility of the police, specifically, New Scotland Yard. The corruption stories of police officers and their arrest at the hands of their colleagues have left an ugly blot on its record. There are many instances where the police have arrested their colleagues in corruption cases.

The newly appointed commissioner of the UK police asserts that corruption is "in no way endemic" in the force. He admits that his force is facing a challenging time following the abrupt resignation of Commander Sir Paul Stephenson and his subordinate, John Yates over the phone espionage and corruption scandals. The Independent Police Complaints Commission (IPCC) has recently published a comprehensive report regarding the corruption of the UK's police officers.

The report admits that allegations of corruption against police officers have severely damaged the police force's reputation. The above-mentioned non-professional way of tackling crime and jihadism has resulted in the spread of violent extremism across the country. Last year, six British nationals of Pakistani origin were arrested by the counter-terrorism department in Birmingham in relation to their anti-state activities. In Northern Ireland, three men were questioned after police recovered a bomb. Every week and every month violent extremists are arrested and released shortly thereafter.

Britain has become the centre of the world's most dangerous terror groups and more than 400 war criminals who often threaten their opponents via e-mail and telephone. Security agencies and the police have been less than successful in countering their unlawful activities. Racism has badly damaged the police department. Ethno Research and Consultancy, in its survey, supports my argument about racism and race equality. In his Daily Mail article, James Slacks is right in saying that, "Tolerance was clearly never meant to mean that Britain should allow those with roots outside the country to flout human rights and the laws of the land on the pretext that things were done differently where they came from."

This country was founded on cultural diversity, but colors still need to be mixed. Though British society is colorful and beautiful, each color confronts another. Tolerance is disappearing, extremist tendencies prevail and racism has become a cancerous disease. Minority communities and the white working class complain that they have not been heard properly. The relationship between different communities and the police must be harmonious. The trust of the community should be restored because poor communication has been part of the problem.

There are many unresolved issues the police still need to tackle professionally. If the police cannot guard a small country like Britain with more than 39 constabularies, 136,365 officers, 16,200 police community support officers and 75,408 other staff across England, how can hope of good governance, peace and a crime-free society be accomplished? The ineffective policies of some politicians, community leaders, religious clerics and extremist groups are leading British society towards social disintegration.

## Scotland Yard, CONTEST and National Security

Scotland Yard is a professional police force with a brilliant reputation across the world but the recent illegal phone-hacking scandal in the UK is considered to be a great intelligence failure as several officers from New Scotland Yard were found involved. Those who hacked the voice-mails and phones of the 7/7 victims, Sara Payne (whose eight-year-old daughter Sarah was abducted and murdered in July 2000) and soldiers killed in Afghanistan brought great shame to the country. The London police chief resigned abruptly and said, *"As commissioner, I carry ultimate responsibility for the position we find ourselves in. I did not and that is it."* Moreover, the new chief of Scotland Yard will face questions about his force's handling of the phone hacking and police bribery scandals. Home Office Minister James Broken shire demanded for police reforms to tackle the networks of extremists and jihadi groups across the country.

On July 30, 2011, Islamist fanatics claimed that residential areas in East London were under the control of Shariah law and held marches on the streets. Months ago, homophobic poster declaring Tower Hamlets a "gay-free zone" was put up across the borough. People belonging to another group told them that if they wanted to live in a country that abides by Shariah law, they should get out and move to the Middle East or a Muslim state. The press association on July 31, 2011 reported Lord Carlile as saying that the UK has become a hub for the development of terrorists. In his recent comment, Lord Carlile said that the majority of terrorists in the UK were home-grown, and had not been trained abroad.

The recent terror attacks in Norway and its links with sectarian groups from Northern Ireland raised many questions as a US-based British citizen sold the "Hazmat" suit to the Norwegian killer, which he wore to mix chemicals for the fertiliser-based bomb. Keeping in view the looming security threat, Prime Minister David Cameron took serious notice while Shadow Home Secretary Yvette Cooper urged the home secretary to review the anti-terror prevention strategy. The threats of international terrorism and home-grown extremism in the UK have recently caused major changes in its intelligence and security infrastructure.

The government published a new version of its counter-terrorism strategy, known as CONTEST. The aim of CONTEST is to reduce the risk of terrorism but the four strands called PPPP (known as pursue, prevent, protect and prepare) have not been too successful as violent clashes in Northern Ireland left many police officers injured in 2011. The intelligence and security committee (ISC), in its annual report for 2010-2011, and the joint terrorism analysis centre (JTAC) warned that the threat of international terrorism was 'severe' but the strength of the terror and extremist networks was evident from the changing levels of security in the country.

The recent arrests of some extremist elements across the UK and prevailing sectarian tendencies have threatened the national security of the country. On November 9, 2010, the Home Secretary announced a review of 'prevent', but terrorism experts criticised the newly updated prevent strategy as it does not reflect national security demands. The Whitehall administration has badly failed to confront extremist groups and their networks across the UK.

The most interesting thing is that British police, counter terror infrastructure and the government are all complaining against the prevailing extremist culture in the country on the one hand but avoid any violent action against them due to fear of a backlash from African and Asian communities on the other.

Political commentators believe that Britain is losing the battle against extremists and the sectarian mafia. Home

Secretary Theresa May is extremely disturbed by the re-emergence of extremism and sectarianism in Britain. Prime Minister David Cameron once said that his country would not tolerate Islamic extremism but, notwithstanding his harsh stand, the PM eats with them at the same table. Experts view this apologetically adapted policy of the Cameron government as a major cause of the ineffectiveness of CONTEST.

Another interesting story making headlines in UK newspapers is the presence of 400 war criminals in the country suspected of war crimes, torture and genocide. Anti-genocide campaigners complain that hundreds of war criminals from across Asia and Africa are living there with "impunity" because the country's legal loopholes are the biggest firebrand in prosecuting them.

In the immigration department, a special war crimes unit recently recommended action against 400 war criminals. On February 4, 2011, The Guardian reported on 383 war criminals including 105 from Iraq, 75 from Afghanistan, 73 from Sri Lanka, 39 from Rwanda, 32 from Zimbabwe and 26 from the Democratic Republic of Congo.

In Northern Ireland and Scotland, religious sectarianism, fanaticism, extremism, racism and discrimination are scratching and biting at the beautiful and colourful body of the state. Sectarian conflict in Northern Ireland has taken different forms at different times, but has consistently been fuelled by extremism. As the most divided society in the world, sectarian conflict in Northern Ireland is adopting a frightening form.

The level of persistent poverty in children residing in

Northern Ireland is more than double that of those in the UK. One in 10 children in Northern Ireland (about 40,000) lives in severe poverty, according to research commissioned by Save the Children. The BBC reported that the number of people claiming unemployment benefits in Northern Ireland rose again to hundreds of thousands.

People living in Northern Ireland suffer some of the worst poverty in Western Europe, a consumer watchdog report reveals. Education groups are concerned about the level of violence in schools, which leads to the permanent expulsion of 13 students a day. The department for education figures show that students were suspended on 166,900 occasions in 2010 for assault or abuse, with 2,460 expulsions. According to a Belfast Telegraph report (July 28, 2011), the number of people made homeless in Northern Ireland has increased by around 1,500 in the last year. Family breakdowns or relationship disputes were the most common reasons for people seeking help from the authorities.

# CHAPTER 6

## POLICE WAR ON GANGS AND MULTICULTURAL CRIMINAL NETWORKS IN THE UNITED KINGDOM

The issue of criminal gang groups in the UK has become much complicated. Young teenagers from Pakistan, Afghanistan, Sudan, Somalia, Russia, Bangladesh, India, Nigeria and European states are playing into the hands of criminal gangs. They are trained, recruited and armed by their masters. In 2007 alone, over two dozen men and women had been stabbed by these gangs in London. Though, the police believe, there are so many gangs operating in London alone, but in my opinion, they are innumerable. As we mentioned previously, there are over 300 gangs with a well trained armed young force, operating across the country, these gangs are involved in drug smuggling and street crime.

These multicultural criminal gangs in the United Kingdom are a threat to investment and market economy. Some have got training from their countries of origin and some have been trained here.46 Members of these gangs belong to forty nationalities. Afghani, Turkish and Chinese are involved in blackmailing, mobile and ID thefts. However, other groups from South East Asian communities are involved in computer crime and human trafficking. As these gangs are involved in drug trafficking as well; recently police arrested eight people in connection with drug crime in South East London.

The London Metropolitan Police Force identified some 183 criminal networks in the city alone, BNP news reported. A news report asked: *"So who they are and how they developed these networks"?* The situation is getting worse. We can guess the number of active members of these gangs over 50,000 across the country. Experts suggest that a single culture based law in the country needs to be amended according to the multicultural nature of crime. The present criminal law needs to be tightened and severe punishment is to be proposed for the criminals, otherwise the nation will have to prepare for the future street fighting.

Violence and knife crime has badly affected investment climate. Major newspapers in the country report thousands knife crime every month. According to some report, there were 60,000 knife crimes every year while some reported 700 every week. The government struggle to control knife led violence across the country has failed due to the way it tackles the criminals. In 2008, over 80 teenagers were killed ruthlessly.

Majority of the unemployed and illiterate black teenagers and adults are involved in knife crime in the country. The government lurks the real statistic about the violent knife crime in towns and cities while there are thousands incidents in which hundreds innocent young people have been killed or injured. In 2008 alone, over 14,000 injured people were taken to hospitals, the figures of killed people are not known. According to the latest heath statistics, every day in England over 40 victims of knife crime are admitted in hospitals. According to the hospital admission data:

*"assaults and injuries from knives and sharp implements, together with sword and dagger injuries, resulted in 12,340 people being admitted last year—446 of who were no older than 14.This is an increase of 19 per cent on the 10,372 admissions five years ago".*

The latest figures from Northern Ireland and Scotland bring the total number of victims in Britain to 13,795 each year."While Guardian reported on 20 March 2007, Up to 60,000 young people, "mostly male, are stabbed and injured each year, the equivalent of more than 160 victims a day.

The Kurdish and Turkish communities are in control of drug trade in some areas. As per their involvement in various crimes and their criminal record in their countries of origin, they are trained gangsters. The Asian, Colombian and Arabs who are wealthy criminals have political links with their groups in their countries of origin. In Asian criminal gang groups, Chinese Triad with 5,500 memberships, involved in hacking, computer crime, gambling and fraud.

Vietnamese gangs, with the membership of 500 youngsters are involved in smuggling. Nigerian and the gangs of Ghana (1,500 members) are masters of fraud. European gangs are involved in the business of prostitution. In London, the Hackney Bombers, Tottenham Boys, Kurdish Bulldogs, in Brixton, Peckham, Lambeth, Abb and the south London Streatham are the most dangerous criminal gangs. In the South, Stock well Crew is operating independently.

The Daily Observer story revealed new thing about the Muslim extremist groups in the UK. The newspaper revealed about the London most notorious teenage criminal gangs who are being targeted for recruitment by Muslim extremist groups. Having quoted Special Brach Police, the newspaper reported:

*"Poverty Driven Children, from Brixton, the Muslim Boys, from Camber well, and the Money Crew, from Hackney, were three gangs identified at a Scotland Yard meeting last month. All were thought to have members who claimed to be radical converts."*

Moreover, all these gangs are operating in London, Birmingham, Bradford, Manchester, Liverpool, Leeds, Bristol, Glasgow and Nottingham. Terror experts are of the opinion that terror and extremist groups in the country can use these groups in their criminal activities in near future. In 2007, with the participation of 1000 police force in London, Birmingham, Liverpool and Manchester, in a coordinated operation 188 gangsters were arrested.

There are over 300 criminal gangs operating in the UK with thousands members. The list of the most powerful criminal gangs I received is very interesting. Some criminal gangs are: Black British gangs, Chipset gang oulsdon gang, Chetto Boys, Peckham boys, Spanglers, Brixton Boys, Fire blades, Kingsland Crew, Much Love Crew, Asian gangs, Afghan Bad Guys, Afghan guys of Ilford, Pak gang of East London, Brick Lane Massive, Stepney Posse, Oriental Mandem, Holy Smokes, Tooti Nang Drummond Street boys, Paki Panthers, Sri Lankan Tiger, Arif Friends of East London and the Narco smuggling gang of Afghans and Pakistani smugglers. There are over 180 criminal gangs operating in London alone.

The recent violent riots across the UK and the way the police has been tackling them put the credibility of the police, intelligence and New Scotland Yard into question. Many experts believe that the abrupt emergence of this violent criminal force and their 'loot and burn' action were due to the total failure of intelligence. Newspapers in London reported different news stories about the performance of the Metropolitan Police, surveillance system and national intelligence model during last week's riots. The police was on the run, Scotland Yard still had to recover from the phone hacking and corruption scandals, and communities remained helpless.

The police were slow to react and the disturbance got out of control. The Prime Minister praised the police but said they had made a major miscalculation in their response to the riots. He called on a former New York police chief to help the UK police tackle criminal gangs but the Association of Chief Police Officers criticised the government and said it had no trust in its force. Scotland Yard's acting commissioner said that more than 3,000 rioters would now face punishment. In response to the UK's police criticism, the US police chief said he was a "progressive" man who could lead British policing out of "crisis".

The performance of the police has been very poor in tackling the few disorganised criminals last year. A total of 300 criminal gangs and their thousands-strong members have been running their criminal businesses across the UK for a decade. The question is: why did the police not carry out any thorough investigation into their networks in the past? Home Secretary Theresa May warned that the failure of the police in tackling the riots jeopardised a core British tradition. "Policing by consent is the British way," May told MPs. The London police commissioner denied his commanders were ordered to "watch and wait", rather than intervene.

The new head of the Metropolitan police criticised the tactics adopted by Scotland Yard during the August riots, saying they failed to get enough officers in place quickly enough. Commissioner Bernard Hogan-Howe told MPs that the Yard was now reviewing its use of intelligence, resources and tactics to ensure it has a more flexible response in the event of any repetition of the summer riots.

Police and security agencies are responsible for maintaining law and order but, notwithstanding the allocation of extra resources to the police, the situation is getting worse. To win the hearts and minds of the citizens, the government needs to focus on reforms agenda. Racism in the police department has badly affected its credibility. Muslim communities in Britain often complain against police discrimination and the stop-and-search policy under the terror law of 2000.

The policing community has failed and the police are no longer welcomed into Muslim communities with their present face. There are complaints that the police do not hear Asian minorities' complaints properly. As previously pointed out, because of the failure of electronic intelligence, the police needs to reorganise the structure of old human intelligence. The installation of five million cameras along with a multi-dimensional surveillance system could not prove effective in countering the recent wave of economic terrorism in the country. Security experts understand that the national intelligence model showed its inefficacy during the protests.

The riots in London are said to be the worst in a generation. With the deployment of 16,000 police personnel and the arrest of hundreds of criminals, the crisis appears to be tapering off in the capital. Immigrants from Asia and Africa are living in poverty; low income families face acute financial pressure, while the behaviour of the Borough Councils is too sneering. Poverty is another cause of the recent violence. One and a half million children in the country live in severe poverty.

Asian and African teenagers are playing into the hands of criminal gangs. The 300 gangs belong to over 40 nationalities that inflicted ruin on the country last week. Knife crimes and violence in schools and colleges are on the increase. Every week, some 800 knife crimes are reported. All these weaknesses, the weak performance of the police and the violent culture have badly affected the business climate of the UK.

The Federation of Small Businesses complained that businesses are just shutting their doors. It is going to have a huge long-term effect on their profits. The British press reported several causes of the recent shut down. Some reports indicated that the wrong interpretation of multi-culturalism, racism, inequality, poverty, the tolerance of criminal gangs in educational institutions, the poor state of education, the presence of hundreds of criminals in the country, drug trafficking, women and children trafficking, extremism, militancy, lack of education, the circulation of counterfeit currency, the networks of African and Asian extremist groups and the UK political and military involvement in the Middle East and South Asia are the leading factors behind the recent economic terrorism and criminality.

The growing activities of terrorist groups in the UK have become a bold challenge for its security agencies. In the UK, poor state of education has left as many as a fifth of British teenagers functionally illiterate. Unemployment is widening the gap between the rich and the poor, making more young people violent. Sixty-one thousand people were officially recognised as newly homeless by various councils in 2010. Nepotism, racism and corruption in Boroughs, and the irregular allotment of houses to their favourite people have made thousands of poor migrants homeless.

They have to wait for almost 10 years to get a house. A majority of homeless people are from ethnic minorities. This means that ethnic minority households are, overall, around three times more likely to become homeless. In summation, the future of young people in the UK is bleak as they are becoming jobless and victims of the prevailing criminal culture and mafia groups. Communal violence may further shape itself in a more violent form, as terror and sectarian networks will harm the national security infrastructure of the country.

The lack of institutional coordination and the present complex way of governance may create more economic and political problems in the near future. Reform in the police and intelligence agencies is a constant need while the government needs to focus on the domestic violent criminal culture and extremism instead of spending millions of pounds in tackling the threat of international terrorism. The UK may face more violence both at home and in Northern Ireland in the near future.

# CHAPTER 7

## POOR POLICING, FAILED STRATEGIES, POLICING IMPROVEMENT AGENCY AND THE OLYMPIC SECURITY PLAN FOR 2012

Various studies and research reports have warned that Britain is becoming the hub of exporting international terrorism. The recent debate in British parliament also signalled towards the radicalisation of students in British universities. The current critical debates on the Olympics 2012 security plan, the police and crime commissioners system and terror networks in British parliament, NGOs and government sponsored private security research institutes have raised many questions including the lack of coordination, trust and communication among the police, security agencies and government departments.

Experts view the present security plan for Olympic 2012 as weak. The failure of the police and law and order management strategies and intelligence networks during the London riots, phone hacking scandals and the resignation of senior police officers from their posts have put the credibility of Met Police, national intelligence model, ballistic intelligence and other law enforcement agencies in question.

In August 2011, the UK police chiefs admitted that tactical

mistakes allowed vandals to loot and destroy shops, houses and markets across the UK. Police commanders and decision maker's face the consequences of these tactical mistakes and weak decision making process—the two key elements that badly damaged the historical image of the UK police force. A recent private research report revealed that police officers had abandoned the streets and markets to looters due to the failure of their coordination and communication system during the riots.

According to a leaked review of the UK Police Federation, police failure during the riots was so miserable and its all strategies remained ineffective. The Police National Information Coordination Centre, which works with the Cabinet Office Crisis Management Team (COBRA), neither did nor worked properly to tackle the riots. During the riots, police was not able to call upon community for calming the disturbances.

Police communication radio system, surveillance and airwave failed and lake of sufficient riots gear restricted the number of officers that can be safely deployed. Communication between various police units had disrupted and mutual aid officers were dispatched without equipments. Government had no contingency plan for the officers on the spot.

Senior police officers like Sir Denis accepted the problem of intelligence weakness between police and community. Unless the present policing problems are addressed, confidence of business community cannot be restored. Recent research findings say rioters angered with police way of tackling the crisis. In a Guardian report (5-12-2011), Paul Lewis, Matthew Taylor and Tim Newburn concluded that: *"Widespread anger and frustration in the way police engaged with communities was a significant cause of the summer riots in every major city where disorder took place."*

Paul Lewis, Matthew Taylor and Tim Newburn interviewed hundreds of people who took part in the disturbances which spread across the country. Guardian and London School of Economics interviewed 270 people who rioted in London, Birmingham, Liverpool, Nottingham, Manchester and Salford. In this report, the authors have recorded most of complaints related to people's everyday experience of policing.

Internal report of the Metropolitan Police released in November 2011 also appeared to identify simmering tension with police. The debate in the aftermath of the August disturbances left the impression that those who took part in riots were recorded criminals. According to the Guardian report (3-11-2011), police began to review its tactics for responding to public order events. Moreover, intelligence failure in the Scotland Yard is another issue needs the government attention immediately. Assistant Commissioner told reporters that the police review continue to be a significant undertaking.

The police National Information centre failed to respond effectively. Daily Mail reported (12 Oct 2011) the London police chief, Bernard Hogan saying that former police commander had failed to put enough police in the streets. Having supported my view of intelligence failure, Mr. Bernard told MPs that tactics of the police were flawed while it needed to review intelligence. Scotland Yard, specifically, failed to tackle the issue with a professional way of operation. The police officers involvement inn phone hacking scandals also damaged the reputation of the force who received money for information from the News Corporation management raised many questions.

Policing in the United Kingdom that faced severe criticism from various communities has failed due to its flawed strategies to tackle disorder. Ordinary men complain they have no access to Borough police commanders sitting behind iron curtains, even visitors are not provided with information about his where-about. As literacy rate is very low and as the level of awareness is limited, few people know about the administrative structure of the UK police.

The lake of accountability may further cause abuse of power. Some recent research and survey reports on the performance of police and its role in the summer riots have raised important questions. Criticism on the police attitude towards communities in these reports is understandable because police has failed to tackle crime, racism and violence across the UK. Experts recently criticized the way police operates in non-professional way. Some suggest that increasing public confidence in policing requires the correct identification of community's priorities. A recently published report warned that communities have lost confidence on the police force across the country.

The issue of deteriorating law and order, prevailing criminal culture, police and community distrust and the alienation of young generation is more complicated. Social scientists warned that a new society of violent sectarian element and professional criminals is taking roots through the instructions of underground mafia groups in the United Kingdom. The culture of violence is prevailing and the values of British society are badly abused by these groups.

Drug trafficking culture of Asian communities, knife culture of black criminals and extremist tendencies have created the environment of fear and harassment.

Keeping in view some complaints from communities about the police department, the government proposed that election for Police and Crime Commissioner's program in 2012. According to the strategy, Police and Crime Commissioners will be directly elected at the level of every area based police force in both UK and Wales. In Justice and Security Green Paper, (October 2011), it seems the Cameron government has showed a lot of commitment to safeguard Britain's National Security and in delivering this duty, according to the Green Paper contents; the government has planned to produce and receive secret information which can be used against the activities of terror networks and foreign espionage.

In summer 2011, the re-launch of Britain's Counter Terrorism Strategy (CONTEST) by Home Office to tackle violent radicalization, extremism and militant networks received furious response from sectarian and extremist groups. Home Office claims that Part of CONTEST "Prevent" strategy which focuses on violent extremist tendencies, terror groups and youth radicalization, support vulnerable people and communities. Prevent was first introduced in 2007 as counter terrorism strategy, known as CONTEST. This is the best counter terrorism strategy and most effective instrument for the government, but unfortunately it faced an open hostility from extremist groups.

The third published version of the UK counter terrorism strategy (CONTEST) reflected a new changing terror perception and incorporated new government policies on counter terrorism. The aim of the CONTEST, according to government circles is, to reduce the risk to the UK and its interests abroad. Though the current debates on the Olympics 2012 security plan, the police and crime commissioners system and way of policing raised many questions, but government says it is committed to a better security during Olympic Game in 2012.

The UK based terrorist and extremist groups have established international link with the terror networks of South Asia and the Arab world. Jihadist groups clearly take the challenges posed by Prevent very seriously. They have adopted new tactics, new way of radicalization and hate culture while Britain counter terrorism forces have failed to confine them to specific areas. The issue is very complicated as these groups have already penetrated into state institution including the police and Home office. They are consecutively abusing the system and facilitate extremist and terrorist element in retrieving British citizenship documents.

The improper use of stop and search powers has recently been the most controversial issue in various intellectual forums. In August 2011, the UK police chief admitted that tactical mistakes allowed vandals to destroy everything in London they wanted. A recent research report revealed that police had abandoned the streets to vandals and looters during the last summer riots. Some police officers complained about the unacceptable working conditions that left them powerless during the last summer riots.

In the Police Reform and Social Responsibility Bill 2010-2011, police accountability and governance, alcohol licensing, the regulation of protests around parliament square, misuse of drug and the issue of arrest warrant in respect of private prosecutions for universal jurisdiction offences have been highlighted. In spite all these instructions in the bill, drugs are misused, police accountability is not existed and people experience bad governance.

Telegraph reported the issue of racism in the police department on 11 Jan 2009 that: Specialist crime unit, such as anti terror, robbery and firearms, are seen as "closed shop" to ethnic minority officers, dominated instead by "white middle aged men with old fashioned work practice" and recruits whose "face fits".

The threat to the national critical infrastructure comes from these home grown extremist groups including sectarian elements of Northern Ireland who caused a lot of fear and harassment. Though government is hardly working to counter these threats, but distrust between the police and other law enforcement agencies has badly affected the counter terrorism efforts. No doubt, the primary role of the government is to protect citizens, but its engagement in Afghanistan, Middle East gives no opportunity to the government machinery to play its effective role.

Britain is not the only country that suffers from insecurity and law and order management crisis; all but, all European states have the same problem. In Britain, specifically, since 22 January 2010, Joint Terrorism Analysis Centre (JTAC) realized that the threat from international terrorism has been severe and terror groups intensified their subversive activities across the country, not only al Qaeda, Britain based extremist groups cause insecurity. National Security

Strategy of the country, published in 2010 describes the threat in the following terms:

*"Al Qaeda wants to use violence to overthrow governments in the Middle East to create a caliphate, a unified government for the Muslim world based on an extreme interpretation of Islam"*

On February 5, 2011, Prime Minister David Cameron accepted his country's failure to maintain long term policy of multiculturalism. He complained that this policy is responsible for fostering Islamic extremism. "Under the doctrine of state multiculturalism, we have encouraged different cultures to live separate lives, a part from each other and a part from the mainstream. We have failed to provide a vision of society to which they feel they want to belong. We have even tolerated these segregated communities behaving in way that run completely counter to our values. "He said.

Many observers in Europe support Mr. Cameron views but say it is too late now to complain. The current model of multiculturalism has failed as Britishness disappeared and races hate each other in streets and in their business communities. Recently Deputy Prime Minister Nick Clegg accused banks for racism. Nick Clegg argued British banks to keep balance but complained that banks holding black people back from the last frontier of racial economic equality. According to the Guardian report;

*"The reputation of British banks will take a fresh battering when the deputy Prime Minister accused then of discrimination against members of ethnic minorities in the way they distribute loans and set interest rates."*

Having tackled their terror related activities, the UK security agencies and the police have adopted newly designed and successful strategies and they are in better position now. As Professor David Omand understands that intelligence remains of critical importance in tackling terrorism and violence, Britain's intelligence infrastructure is considered to be the best security network across the world. The UK intelligence infrastructure has been playing historical role in protecting national security of the county. In May 2010, Prime Minister David Cameron announced National Security Council which highlights national security issues every week.

All of its meetings are attended by Foreign and Commonwealth Office representatives, Home Office, Ministry of Defence, Department of Energy and international developments. In London, during my interaction with some extremist groups, they complain that the Prevent strategy is seen as a direct challenge for the Muslim youth who want to integrate in the British society with their own social colours.

They understand that this strategy might re-Islamize and radicalize Muslims in defence of Islam. Some groups told me that government security agencies are interfering in their propaganda campaigns. The same complaints have also been registered by other terror groups in Northern Ireland.

As we all understand that Policing in the United Kingdom has a brilliant record of maintaining law and order but the increasingly communities distrust in the present way of policing is matter of great concern. Some recent research and survey reports on the performance of police and its role in the summer riots have raised important questions. The criticism in these reports is understandable.

As we know police alone cannot prevent crime or counter terrorism and the police performance is ultimately dependent on community cooperation, but the way police operates in non-professional way has created a lot of misunderstanding. Some suggest that increasing public confidence in policing requires the correct identification of community's priorities. The improper use of stop and search powers has recently been the most controversial issue in various intellectual forums. In August 2011, the UK police chief admitted that tactical mistakes allowed vandals to destroy everything they wanted.

Some police officers complained about the unacceptable working conditions that left them powerless. The phone hacking scandals that transmogrified the reputation of the London police who kept too close to the New Corporation management, received money for information, is a shameful story of bad policing and yellow journalism in the United Kingdom.

The story of distrust between the government and police started on August 11, 2011, while Prime Minister David Cameron requested a former chief of the New York police to help his government control communal violence. The gap of distrust further widened when both the government and the police lost the trust of the communities during the riots. Communities complain that this gap of mistrust needs to be addressed and that it must be established how they are to be policed and how the police want to police their streets and homes.

The public is not interested in whether burglaries and knife crimes have gone up or down; they want to live in peace and harmony. This growing alienation between the police and communities is a dangerous development. The public in the UK lacks the power to get the policing they want.

Security experts believe the police and home office are running in opposite directions while there is a general perception that both the police and government are reluctant to share their security concerns with the communities. The resolve of intelligence-led policing has weakened while the national intelligence model, ballistic intelligence and even private security agencies have hardly been able to penetrate into the networks of extremist, terrorist and criminal gangs. Data on knife crime is poor and cases of kidnapping, fraud and violence are increasing. Terror and extremist networks are getting stronger while the resolve needed to counter these groups is getting weaker.

Every month, thousands of criminals and extremists join these networks across the UK. They have managed long-term financial resources. Members are operating in the UK, Waziristan, Afghanistan, Pakistan, Somalia, Sudan, Libya, Yemen and Iraq, often with the best in military training. The invasion by jobless and illiterate Asian, African, Arab and European workers into these criminal networks is a matter of great concern. The UK police and security agencies have been encircled by these forces from all sides.

The threat to the national critical infrastructure comes from home grown extremist groups including sectarian elements of Northern Ireland. Though all intelligence agencies are hardly working to counter these threats, but distrust between the police and other law enforcement agencies has badly affected the process of law and order management across the country. The primary role of the government is to protect citizens, but its engagement in Afghanistan, Middle East gives no opportunity to the government machinery to play its effective role.

Britain is not the only country which suffers from insecurity and law and order management crisis; all but all European states have the same problem. In Britain, specifically, since 22 January 2010, Joint Terrorism Analysis Centre (JTAC) understood that the threat from international terrorism has been severe; it means terror groups have intensified their subversive activities. Not only al Qaeda, Britain based extremist groups cause insecurity. National Security Strategy of the country, published in 2010 describes the threat in the following terms:

*"Al Qaeda wants to use violence to overthrow governments in the Middle East to create a caliphate, a unifies government for the Muslim world based on an extreme interpretation of Islam"*

In 2010/11, more than 121 terrorists were arrested by the UK counter terrorist forces across the country of which 45 were charged, 63 were released without charges and 13 faced various allegations. In 2010 the government promulgated Terrorist Asset-Freezing Act. According to the act:

*"It makes provision for imposing financial restrictions on, and in relation to, certain persons believed or suspected to be, or to have been, involve in terrorist activities; to amend schedule 7 to the counter terrorism act 2008; and for connected purposes."*

In Justice and Security Green Paper, (Presented to Parliament by the Secretary of State for Justice by Command of Her Majesty October 2011), the Cameron government has showed a lot of commitment to safeguard Britain's National Security. In delivering this duty, according to the Green Paper contents, the government has planned to produce and receive secret information which can be used against the activities of terror networks, extremist tendencies and foreign espionage. This information, the Green Paper describes to be protected and as the government understands in case of failure to do so compromise investigations and endanger lives of civilians.

Terrorism poses threat to the safety of the game. Keeping in view some complaints from communities the police department, the government proposed that election for police and crime commissioners is expected to be taken place in 2012. According to the strategy, police and crime commissioners will be directly elected at the level of every area based police force in both UK and Wales. Anyhow, according to the government circles it needs to receive secrets from other countries relating to the safety of the United Kingdom.

Law and order in Northern Ireland have improved and level of violent attacks id down. Terrorists are trying to attack police or want to create trouble for the local administration, but they have failed. Their criminal networks have been disrupted while their source of finance has weakened.

Having tackled their terror related activities, the UK security agencies and the police have adopted newly designed and successful strategies and they are in better position now. As Professor David Omand understands that intelligence remains of critical importance in tackling terrorism and violence, Britain's intelligence infrastructure is considered to be the best security network across the world.

The UK intelligence infrastructure has been playing historical role in protecting national security of the county. In May 2010, Prime Minister David Cameron announced National Security Council which highlights national security issues every week. All of its meetings are attended by Foreign and Commonwealth Office representatives, Home Office, Ministry of Defence, Department of Energy and international developments.

In summer 2011, Home Office tried to re-launch CONTEST to counter violent radicalization, extremism and other anti state militant networks, received furious response from sectarian and extremist groups. Part of CONTEST "Prevent" strategy which focuses on violent extremist tendencies, terror groups and youth radicalization, promises to support vulnerable people and communities. Prevent was first introduced in 2007 as counter terrorism strategy, known as CONTEST, but Prevent is more comprehensive.

A recently published report warned that communities have lost confidence on the police force across the country. Communities understand that police has failed in tackling criminal gangs and radicalization, sectarianism, ethnicity and various faiths syllabuses in schools that taught different way of social transformation. Minority leaders have often complained that police target ordinary people rather than serious criminals.

Ordinary men have no access to Borough police

commanders even they are not provided information about his where about. As literacy rate is very low and as the level of awareness is limited, few people have specific information about the administrative structure of the UK police. The lake of accountability may further cause abuse of power. The UK police have no solution to these problems, numerous deaths in custody show that there is no accountability even after the death of a person.

The government has plenty things to worry about; drug abuse is in increase, black market is dominating financial market and security threats coming from extremist networks have caused headache. Colours still need to be mixed. Despite UK is considered to be a colourful country but colours still matter in the country.

Though this newly introduced strategy can be an effective instrument for the government, but it has already met with open hostility of extremist groups. Because Jihadist tendencies and extremist trends have strong root in Britain society. Terrorist and extremist groups have established international links South Asia and the Arab world. Jihadi groups clearly take the challenges posed by Prevent very seriously. They have adopted new tactics, new way of radicalization and hate culture. This reaction raised many questions that Britain counter terrorism forces have failed to confine them to a specific areas.

In London, during my interaction with some extremist groups, they complain that the Prevent strategy is seen as a direct challenge for the Muslim youth who want to integrate in the British society with their own social colours. They understand that this strategy might re-Islamize and radicalize Muslims in defence of Islam. Some groups told me that government security agencies are interfering in their propaganda campaigns.

Keeping in view some complaints from communities the police department, the government proposed that election for police and crime commissioners is expected to be taken place in 2012. According to the strategy, police and crime commissioners will be directly elected at the level of every area based police force in both UK and Wales. Anyhow, according to the government circles it needs to receive secrets from other countries relating to the safety of the United Kingdom.

The recent ruction between the UK border agency and home office over the failure of border control created more misunderstandings about the operational capabilities of the agency. The media images of this story have been negative. The UK border agency chief Brodie Clark's reputation was destroyed by some media reports while he directly accused the home secretary.

A leaked draft copy of the disciplinary investigation regarding the former UK border agency chief's behaviour revealed that foreign nationals were allowed on 164 occasions to enter the country without check. The home affairs select committee complained about the cases of more than 124,000 asylum seekers dumped by the agency. Ministers and the opposition blamed each other for the failure.

Recent reports in Britain have warned that the issue is becoming more complicated. The UK based Afghani Pakistani and Bangladeshi extremist groups have a direct link with the Taliban groups in Waziristan, Punjabi Taliban,

Punjab, Baluchistan and Chittagong-based extremist groups. According to a Guardian report (November 19, 2011), two Asian British citizens were killed by a US drone attack in Waziristan weeks ago. Last year, four Pakistani Britons were remanded in custody by a Westminster magistrate court, charged with terrorism offences. They were charged with fundraising for terror purposes and travelling to Pakistan for terror training.

They were arrested by the Birmingham counter terrorism unit last week. In the Daily Mail report, we have another example of how Britain based terrorist groups are strong and how they abuse the system of Britain's hospitality. An extremist, Munir Farooqi, running a terror network in Manchester was jailed for life recently. Various studies and research reports have warned that Britain is becoming the hub of exporting international terrorism. The recent debate in British parliament also signalled towards the radicalisation of students in British universities.

The saga of uncontrollable riots and the arrest of a security guard at the London Olympics site this year provoked the anxiety of the US government to share its expertise with the security infrastructure of the UK, but some security circles understand that, with the arrival of a US security team, the danger of al Qaeda, Afghan, Arab or Pakistani extremist networks to disrupt the Olympic games or possibly target US security officials cannot be ruled out.

In police circles also, there are some reservations over the deployment of the US security team as they understand New Scotland Yard has the capability to effectively control the situation. Senior police officials from the counter terrorism unit believe that the deployment of US counter terrorism officers in the UK will further widen the existing gap between the government and law enforcement agencies.

As Britain is under threat from modern terrorism and home-grown extremism, intelligence agencies are responsible for addressing all the security issues of the state. Former director GCHQ, Professor David Omand understands that: "Maintaining community confidence in the action of the state is important.

Good pre-emptive intelligence can reassure the community by removing the extremists and by disrupting any potential attack without having to fall back on the sort of blunt discriminatory measures that alienate moderate support within the community on which effective policing and counter terrorism depends." As Home Secretary Theresa May in her foreword to Prevent Strategy (June 2011) has quoted, security experts understand that future terror threats are coming mostly from terrorists born inside the country. Finally, all sections of British society are agreed upon the fact that maintaining security remains the primary duty of the government.

# CHAPTER 8

## THE FUTURE OF SECTARIAN VIOLENCE, EXTREMISM, RACISM AND COMMUNITIES IN NORTHERN IRELAND

Civil war in Afghanistan brought many misadventures into society. This unfortunate war and foreign intervention exacerbated internal religious tensions and increased in the flow of arms, narcotics drugs and money across the country. Unauthorised weapon industry in FATA flourished and illegal arms trade continued without the supervision of the state. Every year, extremism and militancy get worse and young people become more radicalized. Bloodshed grows and kidnapping is now at a level that broken all records.

The networks of many groups across the United Kingdom can create an uncontrollable situation if they started importing suicide bomber from Pakistan or Afghanistan. As I mentioned in my previous papers and articles that human traffickers are bringing extremist and professional criminals here, they can smuggle terrorists into the UK.

More than 79 Afghan warlords and war criminals were also brought in by these people. These are hundreds of suspected war criminals living in Britain, despite recommendations by a UK Border Agency unit that action be taken against them. A special War Crimes Unit within the immigration agency has recommended action against 495 individuals in the last five years believed to have taken part in torture, genocide, and crimes against humanity or other war crimes.

The 383 suspects including 105 from Iraq, 79 from Afghanistan, 73 from Sri Lanka, 39 from Rwanda, 32 from Zimbabwe and 26 from the Democratic Republic of Congo are security threat and their suspicious activities needs to be checked. A senior Afghan intelligence service official alleged to be involved in torture and a former police chief from the Democratic Republic of Congo, who confessed in a radio interview to overseeing torture. he UK courts have so far failed to convene a hold a single hearing on the subject, despite the introduction of laws which make it possible to prosecute suspected war criminals domestically.

In July 2009, Washington Times reported that Taliban are buying children as young as seven years old to use them as suicide bombers in attacks against the police and army targets. *"The ongoing price for child bombers has been fixed $7,000 to $14,000; the price depends on how quickly the bomber is needed and how close the child is expected to get to the target."* The newspaper reported".

The newspaper reported. The video of the suicide training of these teenagers are available to the UK young generation. They and their families are watching in their houses day and night. These video have left worse affects on the UK school and college going children and cause radicalization and extremism.

Radical ideologies and sectarian identities can be seen as oppositional phenomenon challenging the UK state power.

At the same time the policies of the state which are more effective have curtailed the process of radicalization. An MI5 report, Understanding Radicalisation and Violent Extremism in the UK, publicized by The Guardian, emphasized the diverse possible routes that can lead to an individual being radicalized. The arrival of radical clerics often from Saudi Arabia with a brand of teaching—Wahabi—that many argue nurtures extremist views.

A former MI5 Chief once revealed that the UK involvement in Iraq radicalised a whole generation of young people-who saw the involvement as being an attack on Islam. Although there is a vast body of work on how Islamic radicalization functions, and an even larger literature on the dangers it poses, the development of radicalization is often assumed to have emerged in a socio-economic and political vacuum.

British society is reportedly experiencing an identity crisis: a public-opinion poll taken shortly after September 11 found that citizens of the country felt that Islam was a threat to Western values. Experts urge, Muslim leaders and their allies in government and civil society must move beyond simply nurturing the "Good Muslim" role model and encouraging acts of good citizenship like charity and community service.

Extremists and Taliban seduces children, train them and use them as suicide bombers in Sunni and Shia Mosques, Churches, markets, military installations, police centres, public places, shrines and government offices. There acts of suicide terrorism, whether directed against political leaders or security forces or civilians, have strategic as well as political objectives. The factories that recruit and prepare these suicide bombers in both Pakistan and Afghanistan are involved in the business of import and export of suicide bombers.

Suicide terrorism has emerged as a modern insurgency tactic since the US intervention in Afghanistan and its illegal drone attacks in Pakistan. As in my previous research papers, I emphasised the factors behind suicide terrorism needed to be addresses, because poverty and unemployment are considered to be the breeding ground for terrorism. Taliban forces in Pakistan and Afghanistan represent no specific ideology, sect or religion, they mostly depends on money laundering, narco-trafficking, black market economy and manpower. Having expressed concern over the UK security situation, in Munich Security Conference, Prime Minister David Cameron warned about the growing threat of radicalization and home-grown extremism:

*"the biggest threat that we face comes from terrorist attacks, some of which are, sadly, carried out by our own citizens. My country, the United Kingdom, still faces threats from dissident republicans in Northern Ireland. Nevertheless, we should acknowledge that this threat comes in Europe overwhelmingly from young men who follow a completely perverse, warped interpretation of Islam, and who are prepared to blow themselves up and kill their fellow citizens".*

As terrorists expanded their range of operation, police in the UK now reached private out private security industry for help in countering the recent wave of terrorism. The present deteriorating situation exposed the police inabilities in reaching out Muslim community and the need to find the radical elements that may be hiding within. Recent sophistication arising from increasing threats posed by terrorists has given policy makers many reasons to label irregular migrants as vital breeding grounds for national security threats.

Home Secretary Theresa May in her speech in Royal United Services Institute informed the audience about the recent change in the nature of terror threat in the UK. May explained: "We see the continued emergence of a more diverse and devolved terrorist threat without a strong, directive and commanding centre and joined more by ideology than hierarchy." The issue of multiculturalism and social integration has led to the strengthening of identity differences. The country has been collecting professional criminals, extremist and people of bad character from all around the world, considering it ok to host the most radical ideologues.

Unemployment and poverty is now causing distress and panic, we are reminded that we are under constant threat. Prevent strategy of the government, which work with different communities has not been successful in preventing people being radicalised. The process of radicalization is continued and every year, thousands of young men and women join the movement. Britain has not been successful in integrating large populations from very different societies, since decades. Those politically or socially vulnerable people, who get legal status here, again follow their previous way of religious life.

In the past, the United Kingdom has been accused of becoming a threat to the outside world, as the as American warned that the Britain has failed in tackling Islamic extremism. Expert say that the attempted bombing of a flight to Detroit by a UK based Muslim, Umar Farouk Abdul

Mutallab, is a vital proof of the country failure. The Home Office denied Abdul Mutallab a student visa in May and placed him on an immigration watch list, but did not pass the information to the US.

Pakistan is a most dangerous state for children and business men. Thousands children and young people are being kidnapped for ransom. Kidnappings of Britons in the country remain a profitable business. Punjab is a particularly dangerous area since the 1990s because militancy has spread out from the tribal regions to Punjab. "Kidnappings in Pakistan are carried out by Pakistani militants, separatists, professional criminal groups and inexperienced and desperate criminal individuals.

The recent statement of the United States security agencies provide us evidence of leT's presence in Europe and the broader Asia-Pacific region. The LeT has established its network in Britain major cities and it has trained militants in Canada and in the United States. According to a recent report, Lashkar-e-Taiba's own leaders, the organisation has more than 10,000 trained militants, 7000 of which are active in Indian-controlled Kashmir.

Though the government is trying to eliminate the threat of Pakistan based terror groups' networks here, but Muslim communities do not wish to stop helping these groups within the UK. Terrorism has an irksome history in the UK. There is a continuing domestic threat but the most serious it faces is from international terrorism. In January 2011, British Transport Police cancelled leave and called in extra officers after intelligence was received that terrorists could be planning attacks. Telegraph reported.

There have been two incidents of terror attempt in Europe. On December 11 a suicide bomber blew himself up in Stockholm, In Copenhagen, Denmark, police arrested three men with a submachine gun, silencer and ammunition who were allegedly planning a Mumbai-style shooting spree. Both plots were linked to Britain, because both the terrorists were living in the country.

An interesting new story recently appeared in newspapers about the induction of young women into the business of suicide terrorism in both Pakistan and Russia seems to be more formidable. In a Russian railway station, a Muslim woman suicide bomber killed many innocent people. In a recent letter, Home Secretary of Punjab province to the Law Enforcement Agencies warned that female bomber may be wearing a burqa. Another sad story appeared in local newspapers about the hired suicide bombers for the settlement of political, commercial and religious disputes created alarming situation in Pakistan.

In the past, the world's most ruthless terrorist group, al Qaeda, provided Asian groups training, know how, funding and justification to mount mass fatality attacks. In 2008, as London Evening Standard reported four police officers in Britain's top force put under close secret service surveillance by MI5 after being identified as Al Qaeda.

The suspected spies, the newspaper reported, used methods similar to those employed by the IRA in the 1970s as they infiltrated the police and the Army in Northern Ireland. All four officers were Asians living in London. James Brandon, Terrorism Monitor Volume: 7 Issue: 9, reported that in March 2009, police in Bangladesh discovered a bomb factory in a Madrassa, funded by the UK charity of Dr. Faisal

Mustafa. Although the charity was based in the UK, British police did not make any arrests relating to the case.

"The news that the madrassa was apparently run and funded from the UK had wider implications beyond Bangladesh over 500,000 Muslims of Bangladeshi origin have British citizenship in the UK and as a result enjoy visa-free travel to the United States, Europe and elsewhere." Terrorism Monitor reported. The case of the Green Crescent Charity, Terrorism Monitor reported, came as the British government already concerned about the possible links between British Islamists and militant groups in Bangladesh.

It is not accepted by most Muslims. Second, the terrorists brand the current governments of many Muslim states as 'apostate'—that is as having turned away from true Islam—on the basis that those states do not conform to the terrorists' idea of how a Muslim state should be run. By labelling existing Muslim states in this way, the terrorists believe they can justify taking violent action against the governments and citizens of those states, even though they are coreligionists.

Third, the terrorists seek to remove what they believe are un-Islamic and alien 'Western' influences from the Muslim world. This approach includes resistance to secular institutions, to certain human rights, and to Muslim religious practices of which they disapprove. Fourth, the terrorists argue that Islam itself is facing an active, sustained, and long-term attack from what they characterise as the Christian and Jewish inspired, but secular, West. This illusion is sustained by characterising relations between Muslims and Westerners as a long history of injustices and grievances, whilst downplaying any evidence to the contrary.

These claims are used to justify indiscriminate attacks against ordinary innocent. Taken together, these four elements amount to an intolerant pursuit of narrowly framed beliefs, coupled with an implacable hostility to the West and its peoples—and to Muslims whose religious practices diverge from their own—and a rejection of basic human rights and values, backed up by a willingness to commit extreme violence in pursuit of their aims. Al Qaida, led by Osama Bin Laden and his deputy Ayman Al Zawahiri, is a radical Islamist terrorist network that particularly espouses these views."

On pages 15-16, the UK strategy report has described the UK support for Muslims across the world in these words: "Over the last five years, bilaterally and through other organisations, the UK Government has provided over £5.5 billion in international development assistance to much of the Muslim world." Moreover, the United Kingdom supports Pakistan, Kashmir, Afghanistan, Turkey, Palestine, Kosovo, Bosnia, Darfur, Iraq and Somalia. Police in the UK understands that the threat to the UK from terrorism remains real and serious.

The police inculcate that everyone has a role to play in fighting terrorism. In February 2011, the MET Police launched a counter-terrorism campaign in the Hounslow borough where millions of London householders being told that one phone call could save lives. Police understand the importance of public role in helping them and security services in fighting terrorism. Residents were encouraged to contact the confidential Anti-Terrorist Hotline if they see any activity or behaviour that is suspicious.

# CHAPTER 9

## COMMUNAL VIOLENCE, MILITANCY AND RACISM

The future of communal violence or civil war in Northern Ireland would be much irksome unless the networks of international terrorism are eradicated. IRA, Paramilitary Groups, Ulster Volunteer Force and Sinn Fein will re-enter the battlefield with a new training and fighting capabilities, lethal arms and well-trained young men. The involvement of international terror networks in these violent incidents cannot be ruled out while the people of Northern Ireland will face uneven situation, more violence, killings, displacement and torture in near future.

Terror elements now attack the police with petrol bombs, blast bombs and use Improvised explosive devices to disrupt the peace process. This is a new technique of violent attack. There are wall separating communities in Belfast city but walls have not been effective in intercepting sectarian or political violence in the past. High

artificial barriers which physically separate Catholic and Protestant homes are not considered being more effective because both the communities members are living in the same city, work there and established business firms. If walls had occurred effective in preventing violent clashed in the past, and then there would have more walls in the business areas to keep separate the businesses firms of Catholic and Protestant business men.

In future, there would be more walls in Belfast but peace will not return to the city unless the issue is addressed on community level or the local state institutions are to be re-organized. The Process of reorganization will gave an opportunity to the local sectarian and ethnic minority groups to experience an employment life. Across Belfast, there are more religious differences between the two sectarian communities and, as experts say divide in the loyalties of law enforcement agencies cannot be ruled out as they belong to the same sects. These violent incidents of sectarian violence embarrassed the government stabilization process.

In June 2011, more than four hundred sectarian elements attacked the police, houses, shops and government installations with petrol and paint bombs. Officers responded by firing 66 baton rounds and water cannon. Masked men whose identity were not known attacked the police vehicles and firing directly on the police. These organized attacks on police and resident areas show that sectarian terrorists have received advanced military training and there might be terror elements in their ranks.

Young children of sectarian parents are a bigger security problem as the go violent on both sides. These young and newly trained people have made security situations in Northern Ireland complicated. As these terror elements are attacking police and government installations, the possibilities of their contacts with international terror networks, either in Pakistan, Waziristan or Afghanistan cannot be ruled out.

In May 2010 and 2011, there have been violent attacks on the police and expert say that was linked to an ongoing feud between Loyalist fractions. The province still tends to be considered violence infected in the print and electronic media because government and its security institutions extensively focussed on international terrorism in Afghanistan, Pakistan and the Arab world.

As terror and extremist networks re-entered the province with military expertise Police stations have been put on a tight security regime with barricades, fences and windowless walls. For a better and effective fight against these violence insurgencies in Northern Ireland, the underground networks of sectarian and non-sectarian groups needed to be undermined. Attacks on Muslim women in both Glasgow and Northern Ireland are another issue of social concern.

In view of all these violent incidents, a question does raise concerns about the collapse of political settlement in Northern Ireland. Recently, sectarian elements re-emerged with growing expertise in the use of Improvised Explosive Devices. They re-Emerged and brought with them experience in terrorist techniques. Segregation between the Protestant and Catholic communities is a future danger of communal violence. Sectarian violence in Northern Ireland has reached on it heights while communities are being separated by walls and peace lines. This is the first way of conflict resolution in modern world. Some religious experts recently expressed some reservation about the thirty to forty walls that have divided communities of Northern Ireland on forty pockets.

As I have already stated in my articles and research papers that violence will spread to all parts of Ireland if the issue is not tackled on community level. On June 21, 22 and 23, 2011, Guardian reported sectarian clashes involving hundreds dissidents in Belfast city. In June 2011, before the Belfast sectarian clashes, in one of my articles (the Future of Terrorism in the UK), published in Daily Times, Pakistan, I warned the government about the intensity of violence in future.

During the Belfast violence, Guardian reported officers saying shots, petrol bombs, fireworks, bricks, stones and smoke bombs were fired as violence broke out in the Lower Newtownards Road and Short Strand areas. The Police Service of Northern Ireland (PSNI) confirmed officers fired a number of AEP or stun-grenade rounds. The newspaper reported. The role the Churches should play was not played in post-violence reconstruction. The conflict is over because the major organized forces that pursued it for three decades. The incident is a lesson in how the availability of weapons has changed the political calculus of militia violence. The use of fire arms was therefore highly regulated by the IRA leadership during the conflict.

The Queen's historic visit to Northern Ireland caused no change in the mind and thought of dissidents and sectarian elements. They continued attacks on police and houses. After her visit, some expected that there will be no more war or violence in the provinces, but the June 2011 attacks proved that international terror networks don't want peaceful environment in Northern Ireland. In Britain's one hundred years history, this was her first visit.

Segregation between the Protestant and Catholic communities is a future danger of communal violence. Sectarian violence in Northern Ireland has reached on it heights while communities are being separated by walls and peace lines. This is the first way of conflict resolution in modern world. As David Mckittrick understands:

*In the West and North of the city, the most violent areas during the troubles, these walls still delineate neighbourhoods. Most of them are ugly, although a few, for example around Ardoyne, have been prettified and artfully camouflaged with shrubs and climbing plants. Sometimes these are sardonically referred to as "designer peace lines."*

In a society where hate, sneer and violent dislike cross its limits, no iron or clay wall can intercept clashed and bloodshed. Recent violent attacks on various communities and their expulsion from their houses indicate that the wave of violence still exist in the country. The deteriorating security situation in Northern Ireland has become a big challenge for both the government and security agencies. Chief Constable of Northern Ireland once demanded more than £200m extra money for fighting against the dissident republican terror groups.

Chief Constable told members the policing board that defeating IRA needed more funds. On 18 February 2011, Daily Telegraph reported Northern Ireland's Chief Constable saying," almost a quarter of a billion pounds of extra security funding will give momentum in the battle against terrorism, Extra detectives, more equipment and ground and air transport will be secured following the agreement between the Treasury and Northern Ireland Executive. A total of £199.5 million will come from London and £45 million from the Executive's reserves over the next four years," he said.

In Northern Ireland, sectarian violence and its waves are still felt in the region, which affected life and society. The recent expulsion of some European families from the region indicates that violent culture still existed. Head of the Northern Ireland Police Federation demanded more officers in tackling violent sectarianism last year but Chief Constable said more people were charged in terrorism offences and the pressure would continue with an increased street presence. The chairman of the Northern Ireland Affairs Committee at the House of Commons, Laurence Robertson, said he was pleased the extra money had been provided.

In January 2006, Scottish Executive published an action plan on tackling the issue of sectarianism. The same year, Home Office published the Respect Action Plan for tackling anti social behaviour. All these actions and steps couldn't prove effective, because the basic roots of extremism were not properly addressed. Since 1999, the government became active in addressing the scourge of sectarianism in Scotland.

In 1909, there were riots for weeks where both the sects fought each other. The whole period of nineteenth century cover the events of sectarian violence took place in Liverpool. The conflict in Northern Ireland has been both ethnic and sectarian, but the struggle of independent state is no more existed. The two Christian sects have some religious standpoints and interpretations, due to which their rivalry resulted in the killing of each other members. Stefan Wolff (2002), in his research analysis understands that:

The issue of racism and sectarianism in the United Kingdom, specifically, in Northern Ireland, has become a big problem for the security agencies and the police. As BBC Radio reported, *"more than one hundred families left their homes in Belfast due to the fear of racist attacks."* The presence of Indian, Chinese and other Asian communities and their religious affiliation can be seen as matter of concern. During the ceasefire period, thousands residents came back to their towns but some racist elements further created more problems in the region. On July 2, 2009, in Belfast, attacks were carried out against the Romanian communities.

Several families of the community fled their homes. This created mistrust among communities and the government in power. In 2006, there were annual plan for implementation of the real equality strategy but no result and outcome reported. The incident reported by the police in Northern Ireland listed the following communities living in Ireland: Black African, Pakistani, Indian, Bangladeshi, Chinese and European. Palestinian, Arab, Iranian, Afghani and Turkish communities are in numbers there. On the issue of sectarian violence and racism in Northern Ireland, there has been no specific survey or investigative report that reflects the real view of the residents.

In the past, in every four people one experienced verbal abuse or physical attack. Young people experienced more violence. There are several political parties in Northern Ireland have both ethnic and religious affiliation. In this report, we cannot discuss the racist and sectarian attitude of every party in detail. In 1990s, the situation signalled some opportunities to resolve this ethnic and sectarian conflict. In 2000s, the issue was settled through negotiation process. As we have already highlighted sectarian violence in both Scotland and Northern Ireland in brief, we will now turn to some incidents recorded by the police department.

Some experts see the establishment of Northern Ireland divided on sectarian bases. They are of the opinion, that the two sects, protestant and Catholic have distinct cultures, history and belief. They are in one time both Britain's National Security, ethnic and sectarian threats. They use violent means against each other. Neil Jarman (Sectarian Violence in Northern Ireland) is of the opinion, that both the communities and sects hate each other. He understands:

*"Hostility and antipathy, expressed in forms of ideas, beliefs, practices and actions, by members of one of the two majority communities in Northern Ireland towards members of the other community is generally referred to as sectarianism."*

There are numerous sectarian incidents took place in Northern Ireland but we can only note the police recorded authentic incident here. Neil Jarman mentioned of the police incidents recording to show the level of violence in the region. In various areas, towns and cities, there have been serious sectarian violence. Verbal abuse; harassment and intimidation have been of different type and different nature.

On the issue of sectarianism, several bodies and institution have collected and recorded violent incidents. According to the government sources, in 1991–1992, over 1,500 people demanded re-house due to the threats they faced. Sectarian in workplace remained a big problem in Northern Ireland. According to the employment tribunal, from 2000–2003, over 500 people complained of discrimination due to their sectarian backgrounds.

# CHAPTER 10

## RACISM AND TERROR RELATED ATTACKS

There have been sectarian attacks on various religious and non-religious places in Northern Ireland from 1994–2011. The incidents of criminal damage, assaults and disturbances from 1994–2011, have been in thousands in Northern Ireland. In Antrim, Armagh, Down, Fermanagh, L'Derry and Tyrone, there have been 450 sectarian incidents from 1994–2003. During this period, over 14,000 residents demanded re-house and 1,500 claimed to have been intimidated.

The recent violent attacks against Muslim and non-Muslim minority communities in Northern Ireland and, the developing racist behaviour in the police department is the alarm of future communal violence in the United Kingdom. The threat of violence in Northern Ireland is as high now as at the height of the province's "Troubles," Ireland's Justice Minister said. "There is a threat as dangerous as anything that we've had during the 30 years of our Troubles," Ahern told Irish public radio RTE. On 24 June 2010, Guardian reported the latest race attacks in Northern Ireland:

*"Isolated families in loyalist areas having their homes ransacked, their belongings destroyed and their lives threatened is a phenomenon now occurring with sickening regularity. In the latest incidents, a mob attacked two homes in the loyalist Village*

*area of south Belfast and in White abbey; cars belonging to Filipino and Indian families were burned. The attacks come a year after a hundred Roma people were forced to flee Northern Ireland after racist petrol bombings, also in south Belfast".* The newspaper reported.

In another report, on 28 January 2010, the Guardian reported a study written by a former Scotland Yard counterterrorism officer about the rise in the number of hate crimes against Muslims in London. According to the newspaper report of the study, "Attacks ranging from death threats and murder to persistent low-level assaults, such as spitting and name-calling, are in part whipped up by extremists and sections of mainstream society."

There are growing levels of unchallenged attacks on British Muslims in many forms, with the fury continuing to mount. There have been cases of Mosques being vandalised, Muslim students being stabbed on university campuses and general anti-Muslim bigotry spiralling out of control without any rebuff. In Leeds once a bus driver was arrested after he allegedly called a female passenger a Muslim terrorist and asked her if she had put a bomb on his bus. However, in Manchester, CCTV was installed while attacks against Muslim cemetery and Muslim graves were reported. The Brunei Times, in March 4, 2010 reported about the racist attacks against Muslims in Britain. In its report the newspaper reported:

*"Racist attacks against Muslim and other ethnic minorities in Britain are on the rise, with politicians and media fuelling hostility and prejudice against minorities. Muslims, migrants, asylum-seekers and gypsies and travellers are regularly presented*

*in a negative light in the media, says the report by the European Commission against Racism and Intolerance."*

Director NCB, Celine McStravick, in his empirical comment (The Fight against Racism in Northern Ireland, 2 July 2009) has revealed some important facts about the growing threat of violence in the region.

*"It is critical that this treatment of vulnerable members of our society is seen as a symptom of underlay- Britain's National Security Challenges in ignorance and mistrust, which can be changed through education and experience."*

MI5 Chief recently complained about the activities of terror groups in Northern Ireland since three years. Jonathan Evans said terrorists in Ulster use dangerous weapons but didn't mention what counter strategy his agency has adopted? The recent terror attacks in Northern Ireland and the recent recruitment of ex-IRA volunteers with expertise in bomb-making has empowered the terror groups to plane more attacks on government installations, critical infrastructure and police stations. The security services are struggling to get a grip on the growing terrorist problem in Northern Ireland. According to the Belfast Telegraph report:

*"The terrorists, who regard the old Provisional IRA (PIRA) and Sinn Fein as traitors, have no discernible political strategy, and no aim other than to get Britain out of Northern Ireland once and for all."*

According to the Times report, the government has plan to increase the proportion of the budget spent on defeating Irish terrorist activities to meet the growing threat from the Real IRA and Continuity IRA. The terrorists are using an increasing number of different techniques—ranging from shootings and undercar devices to large vehicle bombs. They have access to a variety of weapons and explosives.

The sectarian demand of housing for nationalists and the lake of housing for catholic is another major problem in Northern Ireland. Discrimination complains of working class and their loyalties with labour and union movements are another problem. This issue compelled youth tragically to go blind eyes with individual terrorism. Northern Ireland Council for Ethnic Minorities in its report concluded that:

*"The Province's criminal justice system was blighted by "institutional racism" and those who worked in it had not learnt the lessons of the Stephen Lawrence inquiry"*. Another report of the University of Ulster revealed that: *"Northern Ireland has the highest proportion of bigoted people in the Western world." This research had been based on the survey of 32,000 people in 19 Euro states including Australia, Canada and US"*.

According to a report of the Institute for Conflict Research and Breen Smyth Consultants, there are twenty seven areas where sectarian violence takes the lives of residents. Some sources revealed about this violence may be organised by paramilitary groups. That violence emanates from both sides of the conflict.

On 24 June 2010, Guardian reported the latest race attacks in Northern Ireland: "Isolated families in loyalist areas having their homes ransacked, their belongings destroyed and their lives threatened is a phenomenon now occurring with sickening regularity. In the latest incidents, a mob attacked two homes in the loyalist Village area of south Belfast and in White abbey; cars belonging to Filipino and

Indian families were burned. The attacks come a year after a hundred Roma people were forced to flee Northern Ireland after racist petrol bombings, also in south Belfast".

Having remained under the military protection, the mind, thought and behaviour of the UK police force have become militarised and tackle the issues of law and order in military means. Crime and insurgency cannot be tackled by military means; police has its own way of training.

I think there is a greater gap between the policing philosophy and military led policing in Northern Ireland. The army provides support to the police in every part of world, but police maintain security in its own traditional way. Some experts see the present UK police structure as the product of decades of security policing. The Northern Ireland Secretary once said his government has no plan to talk to the dissidents. *"You cannot have any meaningful talks with people who are not committed to peaceful means,"* he said. Police made series of arrests and seized handgun, shotguns, ammunition, bomb making devices and some vehicles.

The recent killings, knife assaults and politically motivated incidents have raised some question about the intelligence led operation of the police. Population and economic terrorism, criminal culture and unemployment in Britain pose a greater threat to the investment climate and market economy. Investment has shrunken while neighbourhood police officers often warn communities about the increasing wave of crime in the country. They are going door to door to get the support of local population.

One major source of insecurity in the United Kingdom is takfiri jihadism that is spreading slowly from town to town and city to city. In defeating all these threats, intelligence reporting should be based on strong technical abilities. The role of private sector in supporting intelligence and security agencies need careful examination as well. The threat of violence in Northern Ireland is as high now as at the height of the province's "Troubles," Ireland's justice Minister said. "There is a threat as dangerous as anything that we've had during the 30 years of our Troubles," Ahern told Irish public radio.

Not only Northern Ireland, had Scotland also suffered from the diseases of violent sectarianism. Unemployment across the UK, specifically, in Northern Ireland is the main contributing factor behind the recent violent clashes. In 2009, statistics from the Business Department estimated unemployment in Northern Ireland about 788,000. The ever increasing list of people claiming unemployment benefits had raised concerns about the Northern Ireland's economy crashing like never before.

In 2008-2009, 18,000 people were recorded homeless, 6,000 of whom had dependent children. Children brought up in poverty in the region risk being drawn into continuing political violence, University of Ulster social policy researcher Goretti Horgan claimed. This growing sectarianized and ethicized violence has been ignored by the leaders of both Muslim and non-Muslim communities. Muslim leaders are failing to tackle extremism in the society.

As Europe and the United Kingdom have come to the term with a grim reality of the threat of domestic extremism and sectarianism, every analysis has been concentrated on the movements and underground activities of new generation and their vulnerabilities. An invisible hand is fully involved in bringing them into the business of terrorism. This unaware, alienated and vulnerable young generation of the country is increasingly becoming pry to these organizations and networks.

In view of future terror attacks, Police Federation has suggested that more than one thousands police personnel's are required in tackling the worsening law and order situation in Northern Ireland. These terror and terror related incidents have badly affected tourism industry and investment climate.

Poverty, unemployment and sectarian divide are facilitating a recruitment drive by these groups. These groups in both Northern Ireland and England openly target poor and jobless young people. According to the spokesman for warriors of Ireland, *"We will target the British apparatus should that be in Belfast, London or Birmingham."* Situation in the province is much complicated as more jobless and poverty stricken young people have entered the region.

In Northern Ireland, residents of various counties understand the cultural and religious weakness of these walls, and these peace walls and lines would not be more effective in case of bomb attacks. Some analysts criticise the way government's tackling sectarian violence or insurgency through walls, but some view the police force is effective and unpopular. Police deployment and their appointments on sectarian bases is view a flawed strategy.

Some analysts ask how many protestant police officers have been appointed in England. This is not the only issue of deep concern in the country, Muslim sectarianism; Wahabism, Barelvism, Deobandism, Shiaism and Salafism are gangrenous dragons which are more harmful for the national integration. In the police department, Catholicism, Protestanism and Muslim sectarianism will cause more clefts in near future.

Recent sectarian incidents in the province show us an ugly picture of religious harmony and communal concordance. Sectarian divide in the police department further increased in our disappointment. Writer David Mckittrick has described sectarian divide in the police in his article in detail: "Two aspects of the life and death of the constable, a 25-year-old Catholic, showed how much has changed.

The first concerns policing. Northern Ireland used to have a great many inequalities, including an overwhelmingly Protestant police force. But far-reaching reforms meant Kerr felt able to join the new police service. He was not alone in this: more than 2,000 Catholics have joined in recent years. His family and his community supported his choice—which was strikingly obvious at his funeral, when the guard of honour was provided not just by police colleagues but also the local Gaelic Athletic Association, standing shoulder to shoulder."

Economic deprivation, black market and unemployment are the diseases slowly developed in the body of the state. Private sector has been damaged by a decades long violence, investment climate is cloudy, market economy is very poor as walls divided communities line of financial communication has been badly affected.

The budget cuts further increased in distress. The culture of hate and sectarianism has recently taken new roots in England's various districts. Religious clerics are preaching hate, specifically in Mosques during Juma Prayers. According to some of my intellectual friends, some religious clerics justify the looting of the wealth of non-Muslim, justify their killings and advise their followers that every unlawful act against infidels is justified by Islam.

These are the people who want to weaken Islam and create clefts among world religions, while Islam doesn't support their way of religious practice. These fanatics have established their own schools with their desired syllabuses which teach hate, violence and sectarian religion. The case of Northern Ireland is not too different. In Northern Ireland, there are different sectarian schools, established with their own syllabuses. Most of the children at mixed schools are those with liberal, progressive parents, rather than those from the toughest, most divided areas. Violence in Northern Ireland is in increase and sectarian attitudes are strongly remaining in the hearts of people.

Racism and discrimination still dominate forums of social debates in the United Kingdom. Sectarian schools, academies and madressas teach students on sectarian lines. In 2001, there were 7000 state faith schools including the Sikhs, Muslim and Orthodox schools. Christian and Jewish schools teach their own curriculums. In 2010, in over 1000 faith schools more than 21200 students were being taught.

The use of modern technology to bring rioters to the frontline should come as no surprise to anyone given the way such technology has invaded all areas of life. The idea that the rioting is "recreational" does have an element of truth to it—alienated young people in this environment can be drawn towards scenes of conflict. There is also some truth in the assertion that the rioting was in the main carried out by "anti-social elements". The most down-trodden in society, with least to lose, will often be in the front line when trouble explodes.

In 2010, the Telegraph reported that in the last six months alone, more than 30 faith schools have been subjected to investigations by England's admissions watchdog after being accused of breaching the strict code" and iterates a long list of breaches of rules. The recent bomb attacks on police, houses and attacks on Celtic boss Neil Lennon, and Kenny Shiels, indicate that sectarian terrorism is Scotland has also now become a worse problem than Northern Ireland's. As the Irish migrated to the US and Canada, to the English and Scottish cities and to Australia, they took their divisions and animosities with them.

There are clear parallels between sectarianism and racism. Each relies on an asymmetrical power relationship, as well as an ideology of the superiority, and greater 'entitlement,' of one group over another. Thus, both sectarianism and racism emanate from 'a politics of difference. The disparity between the government's response to international terrorism and terrorism related to Northern Ireland raises important questions which resonate with the conference themes, notably; what is the link between terrorism research and policy? Has the focus on international terrorism by both the government and orthodox terrorism scholars reinforced a skewed threat perception? How does a government differ in its response to terrorism in a post-conflict polity than in a peaceful society?

The threat of terrorism in Northern Ireland is considered to be much bigger than France, China and US. Unemployment in the province is another problem. Reuter reported thousands people looking for jobs. The role of IRA members in the drugs business needs more research. Mark suggests that members of the IRA were involved in smuggling marijuana, an "acceptable" drug. It is alleged that the Provisional did briefly lose a lot of street credibility in the 70s when they were identified with heroin dealing in Belfast ghettoes and very quickly had to remove themselves from the trade.

That they were involved in heroin suggests that they had been involved in other drugs previously and certainly it has been alleged that they remain involved in trafficking and wholesaling but not in retailing and street dealing both south and north of the border. This has equally been alleged of Protestant paramilitaries.

More recently there is evidence of the emergence of a network of different individuals specialising in different roles. To that extent the structure of the IRA appears to be converging with the changing structure of organised crime. A network of specialists is coordinated by a central planner for a one-off purpose or for a more long term enterprise. Just as organised crime has its 'enforcers', its specialists in violence, so too do the IRA.

Equally organised crime has its smuggling or transportation specialists. Here the IRA either has its own or buys in a specialist from organised crime, as it did to move the consignment of arms and explosives from Libya. This might point to a centralised laundering operation via a financial specialist employed for the purpose either in the USA or Caribbean. There is, thus, some evidence that the IRA has moved into contract enforcement and licensing for those involved in illicit businesses in both Northern and Southern

Ireland. There is evidence of organizational change, but changes in the organization of "terrorist" incidents have more to do with security requirements than with the impact of fund-raising activities.

One of the most interesting aspects of the IRA is the way in which it has succeeded in maintaining its political priorities despite its ventures into a variety of questionable fund-raising areas. The mechanisms by which it preserves a high degree of integrity and thereby legitimacy with significant sections of the Catholic community in Northern Ireland, Southern Ireland and the United States require further study.

# CHAPTER 11

## CYBER ARMIES, ECONOMIC JIHAD AND THE UK FINANCIAL MARKETS

In 2011, diplomatic ruction between the United States and China over the establishment of North Korea's cyber army (180,000 cyber warriors) became the central issue when US accused Pyongyang for developing such a cyber force capable of destroying vital infrastructure and military data of other states. US Secretary of State termed this development as a largest single security threat to the country's interests. Some recent reports indicate that China has developed a strong cyber army and E-espionage networks around the world to collect important financial and military data from private and state intuitions. The FBI report has estimated the number of Chinese cyber intelligence and spy networks over 30,000 plus 150,000 spies.

In this age of technological revolution cyber terrorism and hacktivism have become a constant threat for the security of state institutions around the world. Notwithstanding the changing face of cyber terrorism, the motivation remains the same. Cyber warfare intensified each year but war against a state can be launched from anywhere in the world. In a recent London Conference on Cyberspace, experts agreed on the point that the threat to information security in the United Kingdom and Europe has intensified as skilled and trained hacker from several states managed to wage economic jihad against the state and private institutions.

In a recent London Conference on Cyberspace, experts agreed on the point that the threat to information security in the United Kingdom and Europe has intensified as skilled and trained hacker from several states managed to wage economic jihad against the state and private institutions. In his speech, British Foreign Secretary William Hague issued a stern warning to countries involved in financial terrorism against other states and said this undeclared war is unacceptable. Prime Minister, David Cameron in his turn warned that this warfare is against Britain's interests. "Please stop it" Mr. Cameron said.

Former Minister for Counter Terrorism, Baroness Neville Jones said China and Russia were certainly involved in this sort of war. This undeclared war against the financial and military assets of the country resulted in significant economic losses. At present, serious concern for the government is cyber threat to national critical infrastructure and the theft of important data from important state institutions. National Critical Infrastructure of the country faces growing cyber threat due to the availability of malicious software tools. In 2010 and 2011, various private and government institutions experienced cyber attacks. Prime Minister David Cameron, while unveiled Britain's Cyber Security Strategy in 2011 said: "While the internet is undoubtedly a force for social and political good, as well as crucial to the growth of our economy

At present, serious concern for the government is cyber threat to national critical infrastructure and the theft of important data from important state institutions, because

National Critical Infrastructure of the country faces growing cyber threat due to the availability of malicious software tools. The lake of Internet security has been one of the most critical problems in the United Kingdom. In recent years, we have witnessed some changes in hacker's way of operations while penetrating into the business of financial fraud techniques.

In 2010 and 2011, various private and government institutions experienced cyber attacks. Prime Minister David Cameron, while unveiled Britain's Cyber Security Strategy in 2011 said: "While the internet is undoubtedly a force for social and political good, as well as crucial to the growth of our economy". As the state and private institutions in the country have already been experiencing cyber attacks against their websites since a decade, new groups of financial jihadists started training their hackers to wage war against global financial market.

These groups are skilled, educated, experts in cyber warfare and have the capabilities to destroy and disrupt any financial network around the world. They utilize their computer skills to hack into servers of state institutions and private companies, and use those servers, unbeknownst to provider or proxy servers. The newly migrated UK based experts and groups have already carried out successful attacks against the state and private institutions, but their main developed strategies are including attacks on banks and National Critical Infrastructure.

These E-Jihadists trained in a well established cyber centers exploit Internet through different technologies for retrieving information but justify the looting of important data as their fundamental right. Financial war between Europe and Asia has now become a Hyper-Strategic Weapon.

This warfare is an integral part of world economic order. It, however, already harmed the financial and investment climate of the UK and Europe. The attack of cyber terrorist on money supply of the region has also faced banking sector with an uneven crisis. This is a complicated issue, much more complicated than has ever been. Financial market and national critical infrastructure in Britain may face an unwinnable war against these forces in near future because both Economic Jihadists and hackers utilize an arsenal of techniques in order to target Britain's financial and military networks.

During the last two decades, cyber terrorists have attacked thousands websites including the websites of the UK government, causing millions Pounds in damage. Now this war has reached a breaking point. To combat the forces of financial jihad, Britain's Cyber Security Strategy was published in November 2011, which underlined the technicality of the threat faced by the country institutions from Economic Jihadists and state sponsored cyber forces. The basic objectives of the UK Cyber Security Strategy are to introduce the traditions of partnership and transparency both across business and with international community in an effort to meet the growing cyber threat.

In my previous articles on cyber terrorism, what I had predicted about the abrupt cyber attack on UK state institutions proved to be true. In my understanding, states like China, Russia, India, Iran and Pakistan have established well-trained cyber armies fighting a tenacious financial war against the US, UK and Europe. China has a significant cyber weapons and intelligence infrastructure in place today.

What is alarming is not only do they have the intent, but they have the money. These technologically armed advanced armies have created a new class of threat which has been termed economic jihad. These groups want to target the UK's banking industry, military installations, power plants, air and land traffic communications networks and water pipes. Their basic aim is to retrieve data from various institutions and target electrical power grid and rail networks across the country.

The emergence of well trained cyber groups are the biggest threat to the corporate information security. These highly skilled groups are collaborating to discover new vulnerabilities in financial market and government-run institutions. As we have witnessed the improvement of domestic security of the United Kingdom and GCHQ has encircled these forces from all sides but they still using different ways of penetration into financial data.

Cyber terrorism are the most serious threats facing the country, London Olympic may come under attack from these forces, but GCHQ and counter terrorism forces have successfully intercepted their violent attacks. Cyber terrorists can place many computerized bombs around the city, they can disrupt the security system, international financial transactions. During the Olympic Game in London, experts believe cyber attacks cannot be denied as China suffered 12m attacks a day during the 2008 games.

Recent cyber technology development and its direct links with economic Jihad have brought about many changes to the financial market and economic security of the United Kingdom. In my previous articles on cyber terrorism, what I had predicted about the abrupt cyber attack on UK state institutions proved to be true. In my understanding, states like China, Russia, India, Iran and Pakistan have established well-trained cyber armies fighting a tenacious financial war against the US, UK and Europe. These technologically armed advanced armies have created a new class of threat which has been termed economic jihad.

They understand they are fighting for the best interests of their countries and struggling day and night to retrieve something valuable from European market and industry or gain control over their assets. As we have been experiencing their successful and consecutive cyber attack on UK's various institutions since 2007, these economic jihadists of South, Southeast Asia, China, Iran, India and Russia now started migrating to Britain and Europe to further expedite their campaign of disruption and destruction.

Their main focus is to attack on control systems to disable or manipulate physical infrastructure and attack on computer networks to destroy important data of important institutions. Britain's Home Secretary recently warned that an attack on the country computer networks is a *"new and growing danger"*. The emergence of these technologically advanced cyber armies including those developing artificial intelligence technology are a constant threat to the country security. The concept that London Olympic would be an attractive target of these well-trained armies who seek to damage critical infrastructure and disrupt the communication system is quite true.

In November 2011, Cyber Security Strategy was published

which underlines the technicality of the threat faced by Britain's institutions from Economic Jihadists and state sponsored cyber forces. These forces have already targeted the UK financial markets including Sony, Amazon, Citigroup, MasterCard, Military and Foreign Office computers.

In 2011, at the time of the announcement of Cyber Security Strategy, Cabinet Office Minister, Francis Maud said that the government is planning how to tackle the threat of Economic Jihad and promote economic growth. The basic objectives of the UK Cyber Security Strategy are to introduce the traditions of partnership and transparency both across business and with international community in an effort to meet the growing cyber threat. In its recent report (Tackling the Cyber Threat) RUSI has warned about the sensitivity of cyber threat but hoped that Britain expert organizations and institution have the ability to tackle the threat effectively:

*"UK Cyber Security is handled by a few dozen staff at the Office for Cyber Security in the Cabinet Office and by the Cyber Security Operation Centre (OSOC) at the GCHQ".*

No doubt, government institutions are dealing with the threat technically, but the threat goes wider and number of attacks of Economic Jihadists on government computers is increasing. Experts are continued to see more sophisticated attacks, as well as low-tech traditional attacks, emanating from the headquarters of Economic Jihadist groups. These groups want to target the UK's banking industry, military installations, power plants, air and land traffic communications networks and water pipes. Their basic aim is to retrieve data from various institutions and target electrical power grid and rail networks across the country.

Terrorist and extremist groups from India, Pakistan, Bangladesh, Turkey, Iran and cyber warriors of China and Russia, Hamas, Hezbollah, Taliban and al Qaeda have trained their members for future economic war. These groups can spread their messages through Internet and even can post graphic pictures on websites. These and other UK based groups can finance or hire hackers to attack via Internet. These groups may have acquired the skill to conduct passive forms of information warfare.

They are using Internet to conduct their terror attacks by employing email and file encryption. In Britain, dependence on computer has been major trend. Information warfare is now a worldwide issue serves various financial and non-financial purposes. Government officials are increasingly concerned about cyber attacks from individuals and groups, with malicious intent such as crime, terrorism, foreign intelligence gathering and acts of war. These attacks raise many serious questions for governments since these terror attacks cause mass destruction.

As the new phase of growth in Europe started and their economies are going to improve, Economic Jihadists have turned their weapons towards their industry and financial market. They have deployed their electronic communication networks and information systems with the broader scope of a competitive knowledge based economy. In these circumstances, neither the UK nor Europe's financial market is secure.

Last year, in world summit for cyber security, experts and politician raised the question of future financial war. Director Computer Network in Pentagon headquarter, Harry Reduege warned about the coming financial war and said:

We have experienced a number of attacks against the financial sector, on the power grid and against our defense capabilities."

Economic Jihadist and cyber terrorists' launch hundred of thousands attacks across the world every day and collect important military and financial data from various government and private institutions. E-Jihadists use cyberspace to facilitate terror attacks, put websites to spread messages and recruit supporters around the world. According to former Assistant Secretary for Homeland Defense Steven Bucci: "Cyber and economic means are edging toward the place where they truly are weapons of mass destruction." In summation, business industry and financial market in the United Kingdom must be worried enough to stay vigilant about their protection and security.

In 11 March 2011, government announced the London 2012 Olympic and Paralympics Safety and Security Strategy which guarantees delivering a secure game. This strategy, which focuses on five areas; protect, prepare, identify and disrupt, command, plan and resource and engage, will be dealt under the principles of Britain's Counter Terrorism Strategy, coordinated with Policing Strategy for Olympic Games and the Assistant Commissioner Specialist Operations (ACSO).

# CHAPTER 12

## CYBER TERRORISM, NATIONAL SECURITY, NATIONAL CRITICAL INFRASTRUCTURE AND THE OLYMPIC GAME 2012

The recent debates on the Olympic security arrangements and the threat of terrorism have raised many questions about the cost and massive deployment of army and police forces in London. Political commentators and community leaders have raised the question that in spite the allocation of massive budget to the police and its intelligence unites, why people of the country feel insecure. Newspapers, journals and TV channels have already reported the weakness of the police tactical mistakes; their inability to win the mind and heart of people and institutionalized racism. The recent research reports of some private research institutions about the radicalization social alienation of young people are more irksome.

The issue of Britain's National Security has been dominant factor in the recent debates on the Olympic security arrangements that raised many security questions. These debates also led to the commissioning of a number of studies in government and private research institutions to help the government in designing a better security plan for the Olympic Game. British army has also prepared its own security plan involving the deployment of Royal Navy's largest ship, 22,500 tone helicopter carriers HMS Ocean in Greenwich for the duration of the game, assault vessel Bulwark in Weymouth where the sailing events will take place. Moreover, ground to-air missiles will be deployed and this would be the first time such deployment is taking place.

All these security measures would be police-led but army will make sure its contribution. According to the Ministry of Defense, some 5,000 troops will support the police, up to 7,500 will provide venue security and 1,000 will provide logistic support. The UK police will also deploy more than 12,000 officers with the operation being planned on the basis that security threat level will be set at severe.

According to the recent report of Intelligence and Security Committee, Chief of MI5, Jonathan Evan called the Olympic Game as huge event and said: "We are going to be pulling at least 150 intelligence staff out of other roles across the services to put them back into intelligence work at the frontline." Security Service Chief understands that terror attacks of more than 200 suicide bombers cannot be prevented and their most likely target might be the upcoming Olympic Games in July 2012. Security Service believes that the UK based extremists groups are planning to develop new ways for all new counter measures. In such a large sporting event, the threat of terror attack cannot be ruled out because maintaining the security of 8 million spectators will be a difficult task.

Government and law enforcement agencies are increasingly concerned about the possible cyber attack from extremist groups, foreign hackers and intelligence networks with malicious intent, such as terrorism and act of disruption.

Chief of GCHQ has recently warned about the cyber threat to the UK security and said the country economic security is under threat. Mr. Loban warned that the country is witnessing the development of criminal market place, where cyber dollars are traded in exchange for citizen's credit cards details.

In present global marketplace, Internet is no longer just about e-mail and website. This machine empowers the growing list of revenue-generating e-business activities. In near future, cyber terrorism and economic jihad will ultimately target all Britain state institutions as it has been a driving force behind the modernization of Russia, China and Indian economy and military industry. Cyber wars in near future are possibly to be based on strategic and tactical digital thrusts and defences across geographical boundaries, where assets are taken electronically, are remotely controlled or destroyed by compromising their digital brains.

Recent report of the NBC News revealed that the London Olympic Technology Operation Centre might rely on 9,500 computers and more than 1,000 to run the security infrastructure including communication channel and transport networks. According to the Director research Control Risk Group, Jake Stratton, "London has become the pre-eminent terrorist target in Europe because extremists' threat in the past had been vague and undefined war against the West" Extremists in the United Kingdom may likely to adopt deadly tactics next year as internal security threat is being developed in a dangerous way by these groups who conduct non-lethal training here.

Terrorists may use computer not only to inflict damage in

security infrastructure but to disrupt the whole communication system. As these groups have frequently stated that they will launch a large scale attacks, there is more possibility that these attacks will be carried out by their trained members. They will try to create panic and fear by using IED specifically, peroxide and fertilizer as they have already used in Norway in July 2011.

According to intelligence reports, these non-state actors have acquired advanced technology and recruit young people in their small cells where they use Internet and other communication means. Intelligence reports in Russia revealed that extremist forces can export radio –nuclear materials or dirty bombs. If they succeeded in their plans, there will be massive destruction in London.

The networks of takfiri jihadists and the interplay between these networks, social and political elements, have empowered radical groups whose spread in the UK caused national security threats. The international dimension of these groups is being promoted by British born radicalized immigrants of Afghani, Pakistan, Bangladeshi, Somali, Sudanese and the Arabs origin to introduce the country as a hub of radicalization and extremism. These UK based groups openly invite young people to their propaganda networks. They train them and use them in their terror related activities.

This remains a central security concern for the state security agencies. The recent media reports about the involvement of British extremist elements with the Taliban in Waziristan, Afghanistan and Africa compelled the government to review the Olympic security plan and keep the police forces watchful. As the threat intensified, there may be more changes in the security plan in near future

The risk of violent attacks and disruption is possible because every big sport game represents a new target for terrorist attack. The main challenge will be the infinite number of soft targets to secure, but this can be a difficult job. Every successive government is struggling to confine extremist elements to their nests and keep the Counter Terrorism Strategy to the four work streams (pursue, prevent, protect, prepare). Police pursue to stop terror attacks but failed to prevent people becoming terrorists or extremists.

No doubt, police have a key role within society in tackling crime and ensuring community safety, but they needs to restore the confidence of communities and create a friendly environment while maintaining law and order. Daily Mail recently reported senior police officers admitted the broken contacts between the police and communities. Former Chief of Scotland Yard, Sir Paul Stephenson has also accepted the police negligence in patrolling the streets of London.

The threat of international terrorism in the UK is real and persisted but Metropolitan Police Authority has cleared its position by saying that countering terrorism and extremism is not a job solely for the government, security service or police, the police needs the cooperation of communities. In response to the police stand point, communities are not agreeing on the way police is countering terrorism and extremism.

The City of London police are agreeing on the point that the threat of terrorism is real and ever present but it can be easily tackled with the cooperation of communities. Community based organizations, NGOs and charities have some reservations and ask if the duty of SO15 Counter Terrorism Command and National Counter Terrorism Security Office (NaCTSO) is to protect the country from the threat of terrorism, why they don't keep in contact with community based organizations?

Citizens of the UK face continuing threat from the networks of extremism who have thousands supporters across the country. To combat these terror threats, the government and its counter terrorism strategies have so for not succeeded in undermining the secret networks of home-grown extremist groups. No doubts, the UK experienced repeated home grown attacks, attacks on police, attacks on civilian, attacks on infrastructure, transport and the use of Improvised Explosive Devices, but a comprehensive counter terrorism strategy is needed in tackling these types of incidents.

Police and security agencies of the country have been struggling to tackle the national security threats emanating from the networks of home grown extremist groups since 2001, but not yet succeeded. Every successive government is struggling to confine extremist elements to their nests and keep the Counter Terrorism Strategy to the four work streams (pursue, prevent, protect, prepare). Police pursue to stop terror attacks but failed to prevent people becoming terrorists or extremists.

The failure of their strategies resulted in the countrywide riots in August 20011. According to recent research reports, following a peaceful march in relation to the police response to the killing of a black guy, Mark Duggan by Metropolitan police service firearm unit, a riot began in North of London.

Police in their turn, arrested and produced 1,984 people before the courts. Among the arrested people in London, some 24 percent were under age while four percent were over 40.

Ethnically speaking, among the arrested people, 42 percent were white, 46 percent Black and 7 percent were Asian. Racism is more dangerous than extremism. Communities across the country experience thousands racist attacks every year. In 2010 and 2011, more than 51,187 racist incidents were reported by the police while the same years, police recorded 31,486 racially aggravated offences across England and Wales.

The UK military industry, nuclear installations, financial and other state institutions are under constant threat from Chinese, Russian and Indian underground cyber networks. China has recently attacked Canada's important computers. In the end of 2010, series of events and rapidly developing threats of cyber terrorism across Asia and Europe created alarming situation. To counter the looming threat of cyber terrorism, many states decided to have some immediate amendments in their cyber security strategies.

Indian cyber attacks against Pakistani state institutions, Pakistan's cyber attacks against Indian trade and industrial firms, Chinese cyber attacks on both US and UK government computers and the consecutive cyber attacks of Russia and Iran against Baltic, Arab and Central Asian states give us a dismal message of full-scale modern technological war in near future. E-mail bombs are considered to be more effective weapon than the truck bomb that can destroy important and sensitive data of any civil or military institution within minutes.

In October 2010, the UK Defence Ministry debated the emergence of the internet in modern warfare in its Strategic Defence and Security Review. Defence and other departments in the UK and US are feeling a strong threat from Chinese, Russian and Indian cyber warriors. People Liberation Army, Russian army and other advanced states mostly depend on electronic warfare, attacks an enemy's networked information system. In The United Kingdom's Science and Technology Strategy for Countering International Terrorism for August 2009, the government has highlighted the technological measures for countering terrorism:

*"The UK Security and Resilience Industry Suppliers Community (RISC) provides a focal point for the government to communicate with industry about it counter terrorism needs."*

According to the Guardian news report, Harry Raduege, former director at the Pentagon agency, said, cyber attacks were growing in intensity and sophistication. "We have experienced a number of attacks against the financial sector, on the power grid and against our defence capability" he said. However, Director General of French Information Security said that he had nightmares about attacks on the electricity system, transport, water supplies, the financial sector and hospitals, which are dependent on computers.

The recent comprehensive report of the International Commission on Nuclear non-Proliferation and Disarmament warned that terrorist organizations have the potential to use the Internet and private network infrastructures to stage a nuclear attack. The report has quoted cyber attack on Russian nuclear network. According to the report, cyber warriors could hack into government emails and private networks, eliminating the need to attack a nuclear command and control centre directly.

Police chief of Indian Punjab has recently warned that cyber-terrorism is considered a serious threat at par with nuclear, bacteriological and chemical weapons. The police chief warned that Indian cyber criminals have adopted computer technology with the sole objective of evading the tight conventional surveillance systems of the Police and Intelligence agencies.

India recently suggested close partnership with the US in cyber security, particularly against cyber terrorism, as the two countries take their economic and technological collaboration to the next level. Indian Minister of State for Communications and Information Technology Sachin Pilot made the suggestion in talks with senior officials at the White House and in the US Department of Commerce.

The recent discovery of the "Stuxnet" computer worm cyber-weapon apparently designed and used to infect Iran's nuclear development control systems, presents a very powerful and dangerous new threat to our current way of life. Links between computer hackers and terrorists, or terrorist-sponsoring nations may be difficult to confirm. Membership in the most highly-skilled computer hacker groups is sometimes very exclusive and limited to individuals who develop, only with each other.

Some experts believe that cyber attacks against multiple networks, including target surveillance and testing of sophisticated new hacker tools, might require from two to four years of preparation, but recent reports indicate that cyber warriors of some states have retrieved these skills.

The initially targeted Canadian government departments are evidence of this. The uneasy questions of how to deal with the superpower's cyber-aggression is one that the international community has not found any reasonable solution. In the absence of feasible prevention, deterrence of cyber terrorism may be the best alternative.

Britain's new cyber threat emerged in a time, while my well researched book "Britain's National Security Challenges" recently became the centre of attention in security circles. Home-grown terror and extremist group within England and Northern Ireland can anytime harm institutional data through their cyber technology expertise. British Prime Minister will announce Britain's National Security Strategy in near future, but the day to day intensifying security challenges and violent cyber threat can badly affect investment and financial market. Market economy has already been threatened by the strong and unbreakable network of black market.

The computer system of the Foreign and Commonwealth Office in London has already been attacked 1000 times by Chinese cyber armies. These cyber warriors are trying to penetrate into the country sensitive computer system and military industry. The military industry and financial management system and its important data are under threat from other cyber networks as well.

China has a planed to use industrial espionage to turn their country into the mightiest industrial and military power on the planet. China poses as a rising star in the world of commerce, industry, technology and science. However, Russia has built a strong cyber army and used it against the enemy effectively. Since 2006, Russian hackers carried out four major attacks against foreign governments.

In March 2006, attack on the Ukrainian Central Election Commission's servers. Notwithstanding its 29,000 attacks, the servers continued to operate. In 2007, Russian cyber military command attacked Estonia. In Georgia, Government complained about cyber attacks, for example, the defacement of President Saakashvili's website.

A top UK electronic espionage expert recently claimed that "cyber attacks present a 'real and credible' threat to the UK and have already caused 'significant disruption' to government computer systems". Director General of the UK Secret Electronic Intelligence Agency, GCHQ warned that: "the internet had opened up opportunities for cyber attacks from both criminals and hostile nations, adding that it would be 'very, very hard' to tell which state was behind the attack".

The United Kingdom is not the only state under threat from cyber networks; Defence Signal Directorate in Australian recently reported various attempts on its military networks. According to a Government report more than 20,000 malicious e-mails are attempting on various institutions every month.

As I have already discussed the emerging threat in my book's separate chapter, Britain faces the real threat of infrastructure terrorism. Threats from other states have made the country vulnerable as well. China, Russia and India have deployed a significant cyber technology and intelligence infrastructure. Its intelligence-led cyber networks across the world collect important industrial and military data. What is alarming is not only do they have the intent, but they have the money.

Cyber warfare is an integral part of world economic order. It, however, already harmed the financial and investment climate of the UK and Europe. Investors are on the run and financial firms operate in the climate of fear. The attack of cyber terrorist on money supply in the country has faced banking with an uneven crisis. This is a complicated issue, much more complicated than has ever been. The main objectives of the cyber war in UK are to cause networks damage and their disruptions.

Over the years, new technology and the global network allowed a new breed of the hacker groups' emergence. Cyber warriors can destroy the economy of a country by attacking the military and financial infrastructure in the big cities. Moreover, businesses, public organizations, and academic institutes received highly politicized virus-laden e-mails from these networks. Information networks of these groups jam TV and radio transmission. They can hijack radio and TV transmission for their disinformation campaign.

According to the UK National Infrastructure Security Coordination Centre, around 300 UK government departments and critical infrastructure businesses have been attacked so for. The growing population, illegal immigrants, unemployment, poverty, racism and discrimination in the United Kingdom provide a safe ground for cyber terror networks. Cyber terror networks and group will flourish in near future and their violent attacks on various institutions can be expected.

# CHAPTER 13

## THE FUTURE THREAT OF EXTREMISM AND INTERNATIONAL TERRORISM IN NORTHERN IRELAND AND ENGLAND

The emerging threat of terrorism and violent extremism has become the main topic in electronic media in the United Kingdom. Most people in Britain are of the opinion that terrorism in Northern Ireland and extremism in England is developing into a bigger future security threat. The networks of international terrorism in the country support terror groups and help them in preparing IED. The military involvement of the country in Libya, Afghanistan and parts of Middle East can cause major terror related incident in near future.

Citizens of the UK face continuing threat from the networks of extremist groups who have thousands supporters across the country. To combat these terror threats, the government and its counter terrorism strategies have so for not succeeded in undermining the secret networks of home-grown extremist groups. No doubts, the UK experienced repeated home grown attacks, attacks on police, attacks on civilian, attacks on infrastructure, transport and the use of Improvised Explosive Devices, as a result of soft immigration and weak law and order management strategies.

The principal threat is from extremist groups and individuals who represent a distorted version of religion to justify violence. Such groups are called extremists. The current threat from these groups and their networks is serious and sustained. The issue of Northern Ireland is going to be more complicated in near future. British Parliament in its 6 July 2010 debate about the terror threat in the region criticised the IRA and its tactics. According to the participants that IRA was not fighting a just war.

Since 2001, the nature of the prejudice towards minorities in Northern Ireland has been very queer. The increase in violence and discrimination has been more dramatic. In recent years, there has been a dramatic rise in racist incidents. In David Cameron's Munich speech, he argues that Britain has failed to provide a vision of society that encourages agency and belonging to all, especially Muslims. Prime Minister admitted that so many Muslim are drawn to extremism.

In 2009, there were 22 terror-related attacks and in 2010; there have been 40 attacks in Northern Ireland. In 2009, 17 people were charged with terror offences, while in 2010, according to the statement of the Chief Constable of Northern Ireland Police Service, some 74 people were charged in terror related incidents. What is important is that despite the large number of arrests, the terrorist groups are both recruiting new members and improving their technical capabilities.

People in Northern Ireland complain that the counter terrorism strategy of the MI5 has failed in tackling the IRA terror networks. As I have already warned about the future terror acts, I still believe that the Real IRA and international terror networks are responsible for the recent terror-related violence. They are now called Republican Taliban for their acts of terrorism. The recent arrest of Irish terrorist, Michael Campbell has set off alarm bell. The threat levels of terror attacks in the United Kingdom have risen recently.

Recent news reports indicate that deadly terrorism again became main headlines in print and electronic media in the UK. The deaths of a young police officer in a bomb blast in Highfield Close in the Co Tyrone town on April 2, 2011, give us a threatening message that international terror networks resurfaced. The police officer named as Ronan Kerr, was ruthlessly killed in a bomb explosion. Belfast Telegraph reported Ulster Unionist leader Tom Elliott said those behind the murder had one aim—to take Northern Ireland back to the dark days of the past. *"The deliberate targeting of a new recruit to the police by these criminals is utterly reprehensible,"* he said.

Police and security agencies are introducing different counter terrorism strategies time and again, but never focussed on the basic roots of the issue. On July 2010, the coalition government with a view to rolling back some of the stringent anti-terrorist laws introduced a long-awaited 'Review of Counter-Terrorism and Security Powers' and published immediately. The government and its strategies cannot prevent violent extremism and radicalization by detaining extremist elements and putting them behind bars. The Guardian in its published article revealed about the government programme of preventing Muslim youth from violence that: *"The government programme aimed at preventing violent extremism".*

The government programme of intelligence gathering or

surveillance is alienating Muslims and deterring organisations from becoming involved to do good work in the communities as well. House of Commons Communities and Local Government Committee in its Sixth Report of Session 2009–10, on Preventing Violent Extremism concluded: *"The current international terrorist threat is quite different from the terrorist threat we faced in the past."* Experts, writers and commentators understand that the UK national security threats and troubles are deeper which the country is likely to face in near future. The threat from international terrorism and home grown jihadi extremist forces is already existed. Northern Ireland related terror threat is shaping into a new danger.

Terrorist and sectarian elements along with their foreign partners are looking for various means to create a war like situation in the province. International extremist and terrorist groups are trying to penetrate into the region. War in Middle East (Libya, Iraq, Bahrain, Yemen, Afghanistan and Palestine) and mass migration from the region into Europe and the UK will further increase in the issues of law and order.

As I have already mentioned in my recent book about the religious and cultural distances between Muslim and Christian communities, the developing culture of sectarian violence and racism has embroiled British society into a multicultural conflict. At a security conference in Munich, Prime Minister David Cameron argued the UK needed a stronger national identity to prevent people turning to all kinds of extremism.

He also signalled a tougher stance on groups promoting Islamist extremism. Racism, discrimination, sectarianism, extremism and takfiri jihadism are the issues that can create a bigger national security threat in near future. Though government and state institutions have deeply concentrated on international terrorism, Afghanistan and other areas of interest, but internal security and concordance need an intellectual approach.

There will be a new and modern type of subversion, because more trained people are joining extremist network. More extremists are entering the country and more young people are being trained in terror camps of extremist outside the country. Small-scale attacks can lead to significant cascading failures in interconnected networked system.

In future, such attacks may well be delivered through modern weapons, Improvised Explosive Devices and roadside bombs. Improvised Explosive Devices and other home-made bombs can be more effective weapon against the law enforcement agencies both in England and Northern Ireland. There are experts of IED and technical experts of ammunition within migrant communities who can help terrorists in their war against the state. Police patrol are to be attacked, bridges and government installation will be targeted.

Though, recently revised national security strategy of the United Kingdom has clearly supported human rights, the role of law, legitimate and accountable government and freedom, but soft human right and immigration laws have caused many problems here. Professional criminals, cyber terror elements and sectarian elements entered the country. All these elements are developed into a bigger security threat. At the same time, national security strategy concentrates on the activities of home grown jihadi extremists and demands an actionable intelligence, but it has less emphasized on the terror finance networks of Britain based extremist groups.

The emergence of newly developed terror networks and the fresh wave of terrorist attacks in Northern Ireland have become a bigger challenge for the law enforcement agencies in the United Kingdom. Britain again faces new challenges as extremist and radical groups are getting stronger, the police and law enforcement agencies are getting weaker, due to the departmental politics and Racism.

The United Kingdom spends over forty million Pounds on tackling organised crime overseas, and over two hundred million Pounds on preventing crisis and conflict, compared with an annual armed forces budget of thirty five billion. The country is one of the global investors in preventing terrorism, but its imbalance of capability to project force, stability, law and order management and good governance is still in question. Bad governance reduces the opportunities of investment and economic growth. The recent wave of street crime, gangsters, robberies and thefts has frightened investors.

Factors behind the present terror networks and their strength are considered to be unemployment, poverty, housing problems, and illegal immigration, the networks of European and South and Central Asian jobless communities, the networks of international terrorism, the changing terror strategies of the domestic terror groups, the police mistreatment of Asian communities, political turmoil in the Middle East and war in Afghanistan. The strongest network of black market economy and criminal trade is the main source of terror finance in the country. Economic and industrial terrorism has established strong roots across the UK.

The present unemployment crisis compelled thousands Asian illegal and unemployed people to shift to Ireland and Northern Ireland in search of job. They can be the best prey to the IRA and other terrorist groups there. Somali and Bangladeshi extremists may be preparing for acts of terrorism, and from which terrorism against the UK and its assets may emerge. British society is getting militarised. Literary and political mind is getting weaker while sectarian, extremist and militarised thought and mind is getting stronger. The literary and political vacuum created by this process is being filled by a sectarian and militarized culture.

The profitable business of drug trafficking, and its circulation in the country towns, cities and villages, the growing industry of prostitution, human trafficking, children trafficking, knife crime, racism, religious and politically motivated murders and the import of criminal culture from around 40 countries, all these criminal businesses have direct or indirect links with the finance of home grown terror groups.

Britain is the only country in Europe where over 80,000 people are involved in the selling, distribution and import of narcotic drugs. Guardian reported the police recent study saying there has been a boom in cannabis production across the UK since last two years with nearly 7,000 illegal farms and factories uncovered in 2009 and 2010. According to the report, largest cannabis factories were found in an industrial unit of Haddenham, Cambridgeshire and 7600 plants were seized.

Guardian reported local police saying Greater Manchester, West Midlands and West Yorkshire had more than 1,000 factories. In another case seven smugglers were jailed who smuggled weapons and cocaine with a street value of £10m into the UK. These smugglers were belonging from Liverpool, Bradford, Dundee and Corydon. Daily Finance reported Royal Bank of Scotland was fined £5.6m by the FSA for failing to adequately screen clients, which may have resulted in financing terrorism. As BBC reported the list of terror finance organizations in the UK in 2001 were included around 1,400 people and 500 organisations.

According to the National Criminal Intelligence report, *"organized crime in the UK is a multi billion pound industry"*. As BBC reported of the 930 organised crime groups in the UK, majority of these are indigenous, British-born gangs. They are involved in crime and terror related activities. Illegal immigrants from Asia and Africa are compelled and pressured to act as drug smuggler, procurer and transporter. They gradually settled in Northern Ireland, in search of a piece of bread and shelter.

The billion Pounds money come from the trade across the UK is sent to the militant groups of various Muslim states. According to the Home Office report: *"The scale of the illicit drug trade in the UK is large"*. It was recently suggested there were 300 major importers into the UK, 3,000 wholesalers, and 70,000 street dealers."

There are many networks in the UK, but emerge time to time. The Israeli fake passport story and the story of underground espionage, all are interlinked. Extremists are getting strong and black market networks are flourished. Fake marriages through Asian and African marriage bureaus facilitate terrorists, foreign agents, criminals, espionage masters, drug mafia and extremist to live here and continue their terror related activities.

These Asian Marriages centres are the main source of import and export of terrorist, extremist and criminal elements into the United Kingdom. According to some sources from Pakistan, Bangladesh and India, these centres busy in booking people for fake marriages day and night in exchange of millions pounds. The owners of these marriage centres are inviting religious extremists and people of criminal nature into the UK through their private TV Channels and personal contacts. They have established Television networks, sponsored by Asian drug mafia, invite people and receive million pounds in and outside the United Kingdom every year.

There are several research and strategic institutions which spend million Pounds on their day to day so called conferences, debates, round table talks, trips and hotels. Where are their intellectual proposals and analysis that could help the government in eradicating the culture of terrorism and violence? Some important stories are turning around the Iranian terror and intelligence networks in Afghanistan and Europe that can badly affect the internal security of the region. Iran trains Taliban, Britain and European citizens to use roadside bombs in both Afghanistan and Europe. Iran's Ministry of Intelligence and National Security has established close contacts with all networks of Taliban and al Qaeda in both Afghanistan and Pakistan.

The devastating future role of international terror networks, extremism, foreign espionage, home-grown terror groups, non-state actors and disgruntled political elements, in igniting the fire of violence in Northern Ireland and other parts of the country, cannot be ruled out. Urban migration in search of employment and the settlement of European and Asian criminal gangs in Northern Ireland is seen by the experts as a greater future security threat.

The recent terror incidents in the United Kingdom, specifically in Northern Ireland, indicate that terrorist and extremist groups have adopted new strategies targeting the national critical infrastructure of the country. As I have already warned in my detailed published report on future terrorism and violence in the UK, Northern Ireland will experience more incidents of Improvised Explosive Devices (IED) and, from food poisoning to attacks on police personnel's, extremists want to do everything they can.

The cheap and easily available weapon to terror groups is IED, they can prepare in their houses and offices. On Saturday June 04, 2011, Press TV reported the Police Service of Northern Ireland (PSNI) examining a bomb blast in Londonderry which damaged several buildings in Brandy well but caused no injuries. This is not the first incident in the province, every week and every month, terrorist groups target either police, security personnel or government and public properties."These explosive devices, no matter how small they are, can maim and kill." Chief Inspector Jon Burrows said. However, a local newspaper reported on Saturday that the government anti-radicalization measures pushed extremists underground.

People in Northern Ireland complain that the counter terrorism strategy of the security agencies has failed in tackling the IRA terror networks. The recent arrest of Irish terrorist, Michael Campbell has set off alarm bell. Recent news reports indicate that deadly terrorism again became main headlines in print and electronic media in the UK. The deaths of a young police officer in a bomb blast in Highfield Close in the Co Tyrone town on April 2, 2011, give us a threatening message that international terror networks resurfaced. This was a new kind of sectarian attack in the province.

Sectarian violence in Northern Ireland and Scotland has created many law and order problems. Recent violent attacks on various communities and their expulsion from their houses indicate that the wave of violence still exist in the country. The deteriorating security situation in Northern Ireland has become a big challenge for both the government and security agencies. If we look at the complaints registered with different councils by the residents, we can realize the sensitivity of the law and order situation across the Northern Ireland.

On 13 October 2011, bomber targeted city culture office in Londonderry. There were no reports of injuries and police have yet to reveal details on the extent of the damage caused. In 2010/2011, more than 121 people had been arrested in terror related incidents in the United Kingdom. Police and security agencies are introducing different counter terrorism strategies time and again, but never focused on the basic roots of the issue. In July 2010, the coalition government with a view to rolling back some of the stringent anti-terrorist laws introduced a long-awaited 'Review of Counter-Terrorism and Security Powers' and published immediately.

There are many networks in the UK, but emerge time to

time. The Israeli fake passport story and the story of underground espionage, all are interlinked. Extremists are getting strong and black market networks are flourished. Chief Constable of Northern Ireland once demanded more than £200m extra money for fighting against the dissident republican terror groups. He told members of the policing board that defeating IRA needed more funds. On February 18, 2011, Daily Telegraph reported Northern Ireland's chief constable saying, "Almost a quarter of a billion pounds of extra security funding will give momentum in the battle against terrorism. In his New Year message, Prime Minister David Cameron warned that security services were facing daily struggle to stop plots that would do terrible harm to the citizens and economy."

The recent warning from the security agencies to the manufacturers and retailers indicate that terror groups have intensified their war against the state. The warning came from the Protection of National Infrastructure (CPNI), which works in partnership with MI5. In the past, terror groups attempted contaminating of food in the UK many times, but intelligence reports say there is an emerging threat from extremist groups in the country. The issue of the future threat of terrorism in the country is much complicated while the way extremism and home-grown militancy is tackled is no more effective.

There is mistrust between the police, security agencies and judiciary. Misunderstandings between the Home Office and Courts benefit terror suspects. Police and security agencies arrest terrorists and want to deport them, but judiciary doesn't give any importance to their statements. This is, therefore, the lake of coordination and concordance among various institutions that allow terrorist to remain in the country and continue their dirty campaign.

# CONCLUSION

The 2011 London riots unmasked the transmogrified face of racist, extremist and mafia groups who organized the burning and looting campaign across the country. They succeeded in their nefarious design by looting and burning properties and disrupting communication system. These abruptly emerged violent incidents were a surprise for law enforcing agencies as they quickly spread to every village and town in the country. To permanently intercept such violent incident, experts again warned that unless changes in British law enforcement strategies and European Human Rights Laws are brought about, such incidents can repeatedly be experienced in near future. These incidents and the involvement of war criminals and extremist elements that live in Britain under the umbrella of European Human Rights Laws, conflagrated relations between Brussels and London.

Last year, in one of my books, what I warned about the European criminal mafia groups and their alliance with Nigerian, Sudanese, Somalis and Asia groups running the networks of financial terrorism in the United Kingdom proved to be true. Recently, due to the European human rights tumbling sword on the head of UK Border Agency, more than 400 war criminals from various Asian and African states enjoy freedom of movement, political and financial activities across the country. The compulsion of the UK Border agency and European legal war on British justice system further intensified the climate of suspicion between London and Brussels while some British parliamentarian recently criticized the way Euro rights law provides protection to war criminals inside the UK.

On 12 January 2012, daily Mail reported a group of MPs demanding the Prime Minister to take action over figures which showed that his government loses three out of every four cases taken to the European Human Rights Courts. This is not the end of the story, in future, experts warned that European Human Rights Courts can plan to demand the transfer of the cases of all rapists, killers, war criminals, drug traffickers, extremist and terrorist prisoners and one day Britain will not be able to respond independently. This rights law has created several social and political complications in the country.

In the past, European Human Rights Courts issued many judgments against the UK interests, but now these courts protect war criminals involved in the killings of thousands innocent men, women and children in Afghanistan, Somalia, Sudan, Nigeria, Pakistan, Iraq, Libya, Rwanda and Middle East . European courts have 47 judges who represent their countries respectively while there are reports that some of them have little knowledge of international relations and judicial practice. Among the war criminals are, 73 Afghans who killed thousands innocent people during the civil war in their country. These war criminals raped thousands young girls and abused thousands teenagers and still have influence in their terrorist militia groups.

Britain has become profitable heaven for European

criminals gangs and mafia groups including Uppsala mafia, Bruinsma drug, Holleeder gang, Mieremet gang, Dutch Antillian drug gangs, Plas gang, Corsican mafia, Unicone Corse, Brise de mer gang, Mad Jacky gang, Cahill gang, Gilligan gang, Foley gang, Romani clans, Romanian Gypsy Clans and other criminal gang group. Italian and Russian mafia is best known for criminal activities in Britain. Police and UK Border Agency are struggling to expel them but failed, fighting over 300 criminal gangs, but failed and now planning to bring some changes in the immigration and rights law in the country. Criminal gang's war on the UK streets and markets is another problem that caused fear and harassment.

Former Police Chief, Sir Paul Stephenson one said dangerous criminal gangs are using cutting edge technologies to outwit a half-hearted police response. Scotland Yard has been affixed to the wall while policing intelligence infrastructure has failed to undermine their criminal networks. Police operations to tackle top criminals profiting from drug smuggling, human trafficking, financial fraud and counterfeiting has been repeatedly questioned in recent months.

Some experts are of the opinion that criminal gangs receive huge profit from trafficking of people and drugs trafficking, fraud, banking scams and other forms of high-level organized crime. Recently, Serious Organized Crime Agency warned that tactic allowed foreign criminals to be brought into Britain legitimately on work permits. Scotland Yard understands that majority of organized criminal gangs are cultural networks whose members share a foreign nationality. In 2011, Police Commissioner revealed that UK is home to an estimated 38,000 gangsters in 6,000 gangs.

The increasing power of criminal mafia groups, the deep rooted black market economy, the presence of 400 hundred war criminals of different ethnicities, unemployment, poverty, the prevailing criminal culture in society, the failure of multiculturalism, racism and trust deficit between the police and community are considered to be greater challenges for the British police administration. The issue of deteriorating law and order, prevailing criminal culture, police and community distrust and the alienation of the younger generation is complicated.

Social scientists have warned that a new society of violent sectarian elements and professional criminals is taking root through the instructions of underground mafia groups in the UK. A culture of violence prevails and the values of British society are badly abused by these groups. The drug trafficking cultures of Asian communities, knife culture of black criminals and extremist tendencies have created an environment of fear and harassment.

According to a leaked review of the UK police federation, police failure during the riots was miserable and all its strategies remained ineffective. The police's national information coordination centre, which works with the cabinet office crisis management team, did not tackle the riots properly. During the riots, the police was not able to call upon the community for calming the disturbances. Its communication and surveillance systems failed and insufficient riot gear restricted the number of officers that could be safely deployed.

Communication between various police units was disrupted and officers were dispatched without equipment. The government had no contingency plans for the officers on the spot. Senior police officers like Sir Denis accepted the problem of intelligence weakness between the police and the community. Unless these problems are addressed, the confidence of the business community will not be restored.

The issue of policing and police-community relations in Britain is very complicated. Some recent news stories of police involvement in corruption cases, phone hacking, its contradictory role after the London riots and racism further transmogrified its image. The police criminal justice system is under fire due to the increasing number of the prison population, unrest within the prison system and deaths in custody. There are different police authorities in Britain and each one comprises 17 members, nine councilors, three magistrates and five independent members, but it is not clear how effective they are in maintaining law and order.

The changing attitudes and behaviour of police officers, which have amounted to discrimination through prejudice and racist stereotyping, remain a disadvantage for communities. The culture of institutional concordance, police-community connections and social harmony has been in trouble since the London bombings in 2005 and 2007. Police intelligence agencies are too weak as they do not know about the thousands of illegal immigrants living across the country for the past five to 15 years. The police and its intelligence have so far badly failed in bringing these people onto their records. The UK Border Agency arrests illegal people and deports them to their countries but, within a month, they come back. There is also no clear strategy for tackling criminal mafia groups. The home office claims that policing has undergone a transformation over recent years and that it has responded to social changes and rising public expectations but communities have complaints against the police's behaviour and its way of tackling suspects through counter-terror laws.

Anyhow, the law needs to be drafted to expel war criminals, experts say might be less effective because the sword of Euro rights law and the widespread networks of war criminals and mafia groups are considered to be a big firebrand in they way of enforcement. In London, last month, British human right act was criticized for providing more protection to criminals and terrorists than law abiding citizens. Racism has badly damaged the police department. Finally, the future of young generation in the UK is bleak as they are becoming victims of prevailing criminal culture, gangs and mafia groups.

# APPENDIX 1

*The problem of Racism in the United Kingdom has once again come under spotlight after two white men were convicted. As Home Office recorded more than 51,187 racist cases reported to the police in Wales and England in 2010 and 2011, the roots of racism are spreading to the remote areas. Racism was defeated and the soul of poor Stephen Lawrence got relieve on 4 January 2012 when Mr. Justice Treacy sentenced racist murderers for 14 and 15 years. He said Stephen Lawrence was killed by a "racist thuggish gang" and said Gary Dobson and David Norris were both Members of that gang. The London Police Chief welcomed the decision.*

## DECISION OF STEPHEN LAWRENCE CASE, JUDICIARY OF ENGLAND AND WALES, R V DOBSON & NORRIS, CENTRAL CRIMINAL COURT, 4 JANUARY 2012, SENTENCING REMARKS OF MR. JUSTICE TREACY

### The Offence

1. The murder of Stephen Lawrence on the night of 22nd April 1993 was a terrible and evil crime. Recently the Lord

Chief Justice described it as a "murder which scarred the conscience of the nation."

2. A totally innocent 18 year old youth on the threshold of a promising life was brutally cut down in the street in front of eye witnesses by a racist thuggish gang. You were both members of that gang. I have no doubt at all that you fully subscribed to its views and attitudes. The covert Footscray DVD with its disgusting and shocking scenes and the nature of the attack itself convince me of that.

3. This crime was committed for no other reason than racial hatred. You did not know Stephen Lawrence or Duwayne Brooks. Neither of them had done anything to harm, threaten or offend you in any way, apart from being black and making their way peaceably to the bus-stop on their way home.

4. At least one of your groups was armed with a lethal knife that night. I am sure you were aware of that. The Footscray tapes, although recorded in 1994, reveal the sort of people you were and associated with in 1993. They reveal not only violent racist attitudes but also a casual and accepting attitude to the carrying and use of knives. They reveal a group acceptance of the use of knives to threaten or harm black people.

5. The brief but coordinated nature of the attack by your group confirms that view. A racist taunt, followed by a group charge towards the two young black men, and then the swallowing up of Stephen Lawrence, surrounded and put to the ground by all of you, shows a deliberately concerted attack. A knife was used to stab him with blows aimed to vulnerable parts of the body: once when he was

upright at the start of the attack; the second when he was on the ground whilst the rest of you were gathered round aiming blows or kicks to put him or keep him on the ground.

6. The evidence does not prove so that I could be sure that either of you had a knife, but the person who used it did so with your knowledge and approval.

That is apparent from the brief nature of the attack in which those who were unarmed did not themselves inflict blows or kicks of sufficient gravity to leave injury or involve them in a sustained attack as they would if this was a conventional plan to beat up. The attack lasted in the region of 10 seconds and then the whole group moved off together as one making its escape. I take the view that, in the circumstances, it does not matter that the knife was not in your hands.

7. The cohesive nature of the group tells its story. It is not as if, for example, one person unexpectedly did something that no one else expected or approved of. You, Dobson, repeatedly lied to keep Norris' name away from the police, a clear example of group loyalty.

8. Whilst the attack on Stephen Lawrence himself clearly could not have been pre-meditated since it was a chance encounter, I cannot accept that a crime of this type simply arose on the spur of the moment. The way in which the attack took place strongly suggests to me that your group, if not actively seeking out a victim, was prepared, if opportunity arose, to attack in the way in which you did.

9. Stephen Lawrence is not the only victim of this crime. His

family, (two parents, a brother and a sister), whose victim impact statements I have read, have been most grievously affected. So has his friend Duwayne Brooks. Of that I have no doubt.

10. Neither of you has shown the slightest regret or remorse. Each of you has lied to the court. I do not punish you for that, but this is not a case where there is any mitigation available for contrition.

11. As to other potential mitigation, it is urged upon me that I should make allowance on the basis that this was a murder involving an intention to cause grievous bodily harm rather than an intention to kill. That is a recognized mitigating factor. However in this case it is not a factor to which I can attach much weight although I accord it some.

The reasons for this are that (I) there was premeditation in the sense I have explained, (ii) the carrying and use of a deadly weapon was part of what was contemplated, (iii) even if you did not positively intend death to result, you intended very serious injury and were in reality utterly indifferent as to whether death resulted or not, (iv) death was an obvious risk in this sort of attack. This is not a case where the division between the two forms of intent is a wide one. Accordingly, the weight to be attached is not great. See R v PETERS [2005] EWCA Crime 605 at paragraphs 13-16.

12. You are both now in your mid 30's but I have to look at you as you were at the time of the crime. Both of you were undoubtedly streetwise at the time of the December 1994 Footscray tapes. I believe they reflect how you were in 1993. There is nothing I have seen or been told which suggests to me that either of you was particularly immature, easily led

or otherwise disadvantaged in April 1993. There is no suggestion that psychiatric or other reports are needed for either of you.

## Sentencing Framework

13. The sentencing framework is clear. All parties, after consideration of the relevant legal provisions are agreed. In short, the law dictates that I must sentence you by reference to your age and maturity at the time of the crime. I cannot sentence you as the mature men you now are. In addition I must sentence you in accordance with the practice in force before the coming into force of Schedule 21 of the Criminal Justice Act 2003 which now governs sentencing for more modern murders.

14. In modern times an adult committing this crime would be facing a life sentence with a starting point for a minimum term of around 30 years. That is the effect of the provisions of Schedule 21 of the Criminal Justice Act 2003. That same Act by contrast fixes the starting point for sentencing where the offender was under 18 at the time of committing the offence at 12 years.

15. I am also required by Schedule 22 Paragraph 10(a) of the same Act not to pass a heavier penalty than would have been imposed before that Act came into force. So, I must follow sentencing practice as it was before the 2003 Act. As is made clear by the Consolidated Criminal Practice Direction [2004] 1WLR 2251, (issued by the then Lord Chief Justice and dealing with sentencing for murders committed before 18th December 2003), the starting point for an adult for an offence of this type would be around 15/16 years.

16. It may be, therefore, that the resultant sentences are lower than some might expect, but the law as laid down by Parliament must be applied and I am constrained by it.

## The Sentences

17. I will of course apply the law faithfully, but recognizing that it is for the trial judge to determine the period he considers appropriate within the legal framework and guidance. See S 269 of the Criminal Justice Act 2003.

18. The gravity of this case is in my view of a different order from, for example, a murder committed by one individual upon another as a result of some sudden quarrel. There was a degree of general premeditation; it was a racist crime driven by hatred; it involved a gang of like-minded attackers; a lethal weapon was employed and known in advance to be carried; the victim was completely blameless and helpless. The high level of public interest in this case is at least in part a reflection of the abhorrence felt by right-thinking people at the nature of this crime. This, too, should be reflected in the sentence.

19. This is an offence which calls for an upward adjustment in the starting point because of the aggravating features referred to above. Such an increase is in line with observations in R v SULLIVAN and Others [2004] EWCA Crime 1762, and R v PETERS (Supra). In this case, were an adult involved and facing sentence for this crime based on pre-2003 Act sentencing practice, I would envisage a minimum term of around 18 years. I must, however, reflect the fact that both of you were under 18 at the time. I shall adopt a starting point of 12 years and then adjust it to reflect the

aggravating features and such mitigation as exists in you cases.

20. In each case, and as a reflection of the fact that the offender was under 18 at the time, I must impose a sentence of Detention at Her Majesty's Pleasure. See S 90 Powers of Criminal Courts (Sentencing) Act 2000. This form of sentence is, for practical purposes, the same as a life sentence passed on an adult. See S 277 Criminal Justice Acts 2003.

21. Next, I must fix the minimum term to be served in each case. This is the period which must be served before an offender can be released by the Parole Board. This is a real-time period and is not reduced in the way that ordinary sentences of imprisonment are. It is what it says, a minimum term of the length stated. There is no guarantee of release once the term is served. An offender will only be released if, on the basis of a stringent assessment by the Parole Board at that time, he is deemed no longer to pose a risk to the public. Otherwise he will remain in prison.

22. After release, whenever that is, an offender is not free of his sentence. He will remain subject to license for the rest of his life and may be recalled to prison at any time.

23. Gary Dobson, you are now 36; at 17 years and 10 months you were very nearly 18 when you murdered Stephen Lawrence. You are serving a 5 year sentence for drug supply offences. It would be unjust to grant you credit for any time spent in custody awaiting trial on this matter. I therefore decline to grant you any credit for time already spent in custody pursuant to S 240 of the Criminal Justice Act 2003. In addition, there is no just reason why you should be able effectively to write off the remainder of the custodial ele-

ment of the drug supply sentence, so I will increase the minimum term for this offence to prevent you receiving an undeserved benefit. I take note of two positive reports from HMP Belmarsh.

24. Taking account of all the circumstances referred to above, the sentence of the court for the murder of Stephen Lawrence is one of Detention at Her Majesty's Pleasure. I specify a minimum term to be served of 15 years and 2 months.

25. David Norris, you are now 35 years old. You were 16 years and 8 months old at the time of the offence. Since 1993 you have been in trouble for dishonesty and in 2002 you received 12 months imprisonment for Racially Threatening Words or Behavior. This confirms my view, (and no doubt that of the jury), that you were a violent racist in 1993.

26. You were just over a year younger than Dobson. I shall make allowance for that in fixing the minimum term, but not a great deal since there is nothing to suggest that you were anything other than a full member of your gang with any age differences being less relevant than the fact of membership, participation and identification with its aims. I do not regard delay as a mitigating factor. That, and hostility towards yourself and your family, arises from your own actions.

27. Taking account of all the circumstances in your case, the sentence of the court for the murder of Stephen Lawrence is one of Detention at Her Majesty's Pleasure. I specify a minimum term to be served of 14 years and 3 months. Pursuant to S 240 Criminal Justice Act 2003, I direct that 483 days representing all time spent on remand since 9th September 2010

be credited towards the minimum term. Any arithmetical error may be corrected administratively. *(Posted by Paul Owen. Wednesday 4 January 2012 13.10 GMT, guardian.co.uk.)*

# APPENDIX 2

## POLICE AND INTELLIGENCE FORCES

There are dozen police forces in the United Kingdom. All these forces and its intelligence networks have been struggling to protect the security of the country since its inception. In this chapter I want to briefly introduce some important police forces to elucidate how Britain's law enforcement agencies operate and what is their administrative structure.

## Police Forces

1-13 Territorial force in England.

2-Territorial force in Scotland.

3-1 special police force.

4-1 territorial force in the crown dependencies.

5-1 park police force.

In March 2010, the England and Wales police force numbered: 143,734 officers and Police Community Support Officers were 16,918 while other staff was counted 79,596.

## Forces in England

1-Avon and Somerset Constabulary. 2-Bedfordshire Police. 3-Cambridgeshire Constabulary. 4-Cheshire Constabulary. 5-City of London Police. 6-Cleveland Police. 7-Cumbria Constabulary. 8-Derbyshire Constabulary. 9-Devon and Cornwall Police. 10-Dorset Police. 11-Durham Constabulary. 12-Essex Police. 13-Gloucestershire Constabulary. 14-Greate Manchester Police. 15-Hampshire Constabulary. 16-Hertfordshire Constabulary. 17-Humberside Police. 18-Kent Police. 19-Lancashire Constabulary. 20-Leicestershire Constabulary.

21-Lincolnshire Police. 22-Merseyside Police. 23-Metropolitan Police. 24-Norfolk Constabulary. 25-Northamptonshire Police. 26-Northumbria Police. 27-North Yorkshire Police. 28-Nottinghamshire Police. 29-South Yorkshire Police. 30-Staffordshire Police. 31-Suffold Constabulary. 32-Surrey Police. 33-Sussex Police. 34-Thamas Valley Police. 35-Warvickshire Police. 36-West Mercia Police. 37-West Midland Police. 38-West Yorkshire Police. 39-Wiltshire Police.

40-Association of Chief Police Officers Vehicle Crime Intelligence Service.

41-National Ballistics Intelligence Service or NABIS is a police intelligence agency dedicated to managing and providing detailed information regarding firearm related criminality. This agency was launched in 1 April 2008.

42-National Intelligence Model is intelligence led business (NIM), utilized by police forces in the UK. The NIM was devised by the National Criminal Intelligence Service and adopted by the Association of Chief Police Officers Scotland in 2000.

43-National Counter Terrorism Security Office.

44-National Domestic Extremism Team.

45-National Extremism Tactical Co-ordination Unit.

46-National Public Order Intelligence Unit.

47-National Wildlife Crime Unit.

48-British Transport Police.

49-Civil Nuclear Constabulary.

50-Ministry of Defense Police.

51-Scottish Crime and Drug Enforcement Agency.

52-The National Criminal Intelligence Service (NCIS) was a United Kingdom policing agency set up as a separate body in April 1992 to centralize the gathering and distribution of intelligence on serious and organized criminal matters. On 1 April 2006 it was merged into the newly created Serious Organized Crime Agency.

53-Independent Police Complaints Commission was formed in April 2004 as a non-departmental body to settle the public complaints about the police. The statutory powers and responsibilities of this body are set out by the police act 2002.

54-The Serious Organized Crime Agency (SOCA) is also considered to be a non-departmental public body of the UK government under the sponsorship of Home Office. This police organization was established under section-1 of serious organized crime and police act 2005. This agency was formed in 1 April 2006 following the merger of Crime Squad, National Criminal Intelligence ( ), National Hi-Tech Crime Unit (NHTCU), the investigative and intelligence sections of HM Revenue and Custom or serious drug trafficking and the Immigration Services' responsibilities for organized immigration crime.

55-National Policing Improvement Agency. This agency became operational in 1 April 2007. NPIA was proposed by Association of Chief Police Officers. The motivation for creating NPIA was laid out in 2004 police reform white paper.

56-The serious crime analysis section was initiated by the Home Office in 1998 with one main objective—to identify the potential emergence of and serial at the earliest stage of their offending.

57-The Police National Missing Persons Bureau acts as the centre for the exchange of information connected with the search for missing persons nationally and internationally.

58-MOD Police and Guarding Agency (MDPGA).MOD Police and Guarding Agency (MDPGA)

59-The Security Service, MI5 is an internal counter-intelligence and security agency.

60-Counter Terrorism Command or SO15 is a Specialist Operation Branch.

61-Joint Terrorism Analysis Centre (JTAC).

## The Metropolitan Police, London

A well established Police organization, commonly known, Metropolitan Police is responsible for policing and law and order management in London. Metropolitan Police was formed by former Home Secretary Sir Robert Peel with the implementation of the Metropolitan Police Act, passed by Parliament in 1829.

The Central Communications Command (CCC) known as metcall is a strongest operational command.

## Wales Police Forces

1-Dyfed Powys Police force.

2-Gwent Police.

3-North Wales Police.

4-South Wales Police.

## Scotland Police Forces

1-Central Scotland Police

2-Dumfries and Galloway Constabulary. 3-Fife Constabulary

4-Grampian Police.

5-Lothian and Border Force.

6-Northern Constabulary.

7-Strachclyde Police.

8-Tayside Police.

9-British Transport Police.

10-Ministry of Defence Police Force.

11-Scottish Crime and Drug Enforcement Agency.

## Bodies with Investigatory Powers and Limited Police Powers

1-Independent Police Complaints Commission.

2-Serious Organized Crime Agency.

UK Border Agency was formed in 2008.

Her Majesty's Revenue and Custom.

## Miscellaneous Constabularies

1-Port Police, operating under the Harbor, Dock and Piers Clause Act 1847.

2-Belfast Habor Police.

3-Larne Harbor Police.

4-Port Bristol Police.

5-Port of Felixtowe Police.

6-Port of Portland Police.

7-Falmouth Dock Police.

8-Port of Dover Police.

## Other Ports Police

1-Port of Liverpool Police.

2-Port of Tilbury Police.

3-Tees and Hartlepool Port Police.

## Royal Parks Constabulary

1-Barking and Dagenham Parks Constabulary.

2-Hammersmith Heath Constabulary.

3-Hammersmith and Fulham Parks Constabulary.

4-Hillingdon Parks Patrol Police.

5-Redbridge Parks Police.

6-Royal Borough of Kensington and Chelsea Parks Police.

7-Sutton Parks Constabulary.

8-Wandsworth Parks Police.

## Military police of the United Kingdom

1-Royal Navy Police.

2-Royal Marines Police.

3-RoyalMilitary Police.

4-Royal Air Force Police.

## Fictional Police Forces

1-County Police

2-Dee Valley Police

3-Eastland Constabulary.

4-East Tyne Police.

5-Midland Central Police.

6-Midsomer Constabulary.

7-North Counties Constabulary.

8-North West Police.

9-Sandford Police Service.

10-Tatshire Blues.

11-Thamesford Constabulary.

12-Tyneside Police.

13-Wyvern Constabulary.

## Police Units

1-CO1-Central Operation HQ

2-CO3-Emergency Preparedness Operational Command Unit.

3-CO5-Firearms Command Unit.

4-CO10-Central Communication Command.

5-CO11-Public Order Operational Command Unit.

6-CO12-2012 Olympic Operation.

7-CO15-Traffic Operational Command Unit.

8-CO16-Traffick Criminal Justice Unit.

9-CO19-Specialist Firearm Command.

10-CO20-Territorial Support Group.

## Operational Support

1-Air Support Unit.

2-Dog Support Unit.

3-Film Unit.

4-Marine Policing Unit.

5-Mounted Branch.

## The Police Legislation

There are numerous police law and acts in the United Kingdom, but we have selected some important legislation to inculcate my readers about the police performance.

1-Anti Terrorism, Crime and Security Act 2001.

2-Crime and Disorder Act 1998.

3-Criminal Justice Act 1998 and 2003.

4-Criminal Justice and Court Services Act 2000.

5-Criminal Justice and Police Act 2001.

6-Criminal Law (Scotland) 1995.

7-Criminal Procedure (Scotland) 1995.

8-Data Protection Act 1998.

9-Human Rights Act 1998.

10-Immigration and Asylum Act 1999.

11-Private security Industry Act 2001,

12-Police Act.

13-Police Reform Act 2002.

14-Procedure of Crime Act 2002.

15-The Police (Scotland) Regulations 2004.

16-Regulations of Investigatory Powers Act 2000.

17-Road Traffic Act 1998.

18-Serious Organized Crime Act 2005.

19-Terrorism Act 2000.

20-The Misuse of Drug Act 1971. Offences under of drug act are possession of a controlled drug, possession with intent to supply another person, production, cultivation or manufacture of controlled drugs and import and export of controlled drugs

21-Custom and Excise Management Act 1979.

22-Drug Traffic Act 1994.

23-Crime and Disorder Act 1998.

24-Metropolitan Police Act 1829.

25-Police Reforms and Responsibility Bill 2010-2011.

26-Serious Crime Act 2007.

27-Proceeds of Crime Act 2002.

28-Extradition Act 2003.

29-Border, Citizenship and Immigration Act 2009.

30-Race Relations Act 1965.

31-Police (Detention and Bill) Act 2011.

32-Data Protection Act 1998.

# NOTES AND REFERENCES

1-Daily Mail reported (12 Oct 2011) the London police chief, Bernard Hogan saying that former police commander had failed to put enough police in the streets.

2-In Justice and Security Green Paper, (October 2011), it seems the Cameron government has showed a lot of commitment to safeguard Britain's National Security and in delivering this duty.

3-National Security Strategy of the country, published in 2010 describes the threat of al Qaeda that wants to use violence to overthrow governments in the Middle East to create a caliphate, a unifies government for the Muslim world based on an extreme interpretation of Islam.

4-Justice and Security Green Paper, Presented to Parliament by the Secretary of State for Justice by Command of Her Majesty October 2011.

5-Justice and Security Green Paper: Presented to Parliament by the Secretary of State for Justice by Command of Her Majesty October 2011.

6-Intelligence and Security Committee Annual Report 2010–2011 . . . Chairman: The Rt. Hon. Sir Malcolm Rifkind, MP.

Intelligence Services Act 1994 . . . Chapter 13. Presented to Parliament by the Prime Minister by Command of Her Majesty. July 2011.

7-The Extremist Reaction to the UK's Prevent Strategy. By Jack Barclay, Published on Tuesday, October 18, 2011.

8-The spring of a New Political Salafism? By Hassan Mneimneh. Published on Wednesday, October 19, 2011

9-The Assertion of Barelvi Extremism. By Ismail Khan. Published on Wednesday, October 19, 2011

10-The Nature of Prejudice. Allport, G. New York. USA. 1958.

11-The Manners and Customs of Police. Black. D. 1980. Academic Press New York.

12-Bland, N., Mundy, G., Russell, J., and Tuffin, R. (1999).

13-Bowling, B. (1993) Racial Harassment and the process of victimization. British Journal of Criminology. Bowling B. 1993.

14-Identity Construction among British Asian Muslim youth. Ulku Guney.

15-The Extremist Reaction to the UK's Prevent Strategy. By Jack Barclay. Published on Tuesday, October 18, 2011

16-Preventing Violent Extremism: Response by the Islamic Human Rights Commission to UK Government

Consultation, September 2009. Islamic Human Rights Commission

17-The police acts 1964, 1996, and 2000 the police act define the area and authority of the police in the United Kingdom. The act of 1964 was amended and replaced. Various sections of the act define responsibilities of the UK police force.

18-The Brunei Times, in March 4, 2010 reported about the racist attacks against Muslims in Britain.

19-Priority risk of the National Security, A Strong Britain in an Age of Uncertainty: The National Security Strategy Presented to Parliament by the Prime Minister, by Command of Her Majesty, October 2010, PP-14, 27.

20-On Sep 24, 2010, CNN reported Britain's warning over Irish-related terrorism. "MI5 chief has claimed a rise in Northern Irish terrorist activity Security Service raises threat level to "substantial" Home secretary announced Irish-related threat assessment balance in staying alert but not alarmed.

21-Cyber Security and the UK's Critical National Infrastructure, a Chatham House recent report September-2011.

22-National Security Strategy and Strategic Defence and Security Review released in 2010 have underlined cyber terrorism as a bigger security threat.

23-In part one (The Strategic Context, page-14), of the National Security Strategy, presented to parliament by Prime Minister by command of Her Majesty, October 2010,

Government has warned that Al Qaeda remains the most potent terrorist threat to the UK.

24-In 4 February 2011, Guardian reported: "The 383 suspects include 105 from Iraq, 75 from Afghanistan, 73 from Sri Lanka, 39 from Rwanda, 32 from Zimbabwe and 26 from the Democratic Republic of Congo.

25-On August 25, 2011, the Daily Mail reported an independent inquiry into the aspects of alleged racism in the metropolitan police department.

26-On April 29, 2011, the Daily Mail reported that a lady police constable, Hina Parekh, had resigned over racist abuse and bullying in the Metropolitan Police. Hinah Parekh said racist abuse from fellow police officers caused her to suffer from depression and stress.

27-Bradley Report (2009), the Independent Police Complaints Authority Report (2008), the Commission for Racial Equality's (CRE) Formal Investigation into the Police Service (2003) and the Stephen Lawrence Enquiry Report (1999), during the last 10 years, is fully implemented then we can expect there will be an improvement in the performance of the UK police.

28-In 2009, Guardian newspaper in its editorial reported that the claim that policing has become dangerously over centralized is now a political commonplace. But it is not just a slogan. Good policing depends on local support, on the willingness of individual citizens to come forward as witness or to support dubious activity.

29-In March 4, 2008, BBC reported twelve more racist police officers were punished.

30-The report of Internet Journal of Criminology "Black and Asian police officers and support staff: Prejudices, Identity, Agency and Social Cohesion, 2006.

31-On October 27, 2008, ANI reported a black intelligence officer was racially assaulted by two white men.

32-On March 13, 2005, Sunday Times reported a Middle Eastern lawyer threatened the UK police of legal action, for their racist behavior, with the Arab communities in the country.

33-Guardian reported on 20 March 2007, Up to 60,000 young people, "mostly male, are stabbed and injured each year, the equivalent of more than 160 victims a day.

34-In a Guardian report (5-12-2011), Paul Lewis, Matthew Taylor and Tim Newburn concluded that widespread anger and frustration in the way police engaged with communities was a significant cause of the summer riots in every major city where disorder took place.

35-On Sep 24, 2010, CNN reported Britain's warning over Irish-related terrorism.

36-On February 18, 2011, Daily Telegraph reported Northern Ireland's chief constable saying, almost a quarter of a billion pounds of extra security funding will give momentum in the battle against terrorism.

37-In 2008, as London Evening Standard reported four

police officers in Britain's top force put under close secret service surveillance by MI5 after being identified as Al Qaeda.

39-The Future of Cyber Terrorism: Where the Physical and Virtual Worlds Converge. Remarks by: Barry C. Collin. Institute for Security and Intelligence

40-Multiculturalism has made Progress in Britain-but white reticence is still the stumbling block. Tariq Mohmood. Guardian 7 Feb, 2011.

41-Guardian, Wednesday 14 December 2011

42-Britain facing home growing terrorist threat. CNN, 27 August. 2010.

43-Radicalization among Muslims in the UK: MICROCON, Policy Working Paper, May 2009.

44-Understanding Violent Radicalization, Terrorist and Jihadist Movements in Europe. Magnus Ranstop. Routledge, 2009.

45-Pakistan: Karachi's Madrasas and Violent Extremism.

46-Policing Controversy, Blair, Sir Ian, Profile le Books, London 2009

47-A History of Policing in England and Wales from 1974, Brain, Timothy, Oxford University Press 2010

48-A History of Police in England and Wales. Critchley, T A, Constable, London 1978

49-The Great British Bobby: A History of British Policing from the 18th Century to The Present, Emsley, C., Quercus, London 2009

50-Policing for the People: Interim Report of the Police Reform Taskforce, Herbert, Nicholas. Conservative Party, London 2007

51-Individual monetary incentives: A review of different types of arrangements between performance and pay. Bucklin, B., & Dickinson, A. 2001. Journal of Organizational Behavior Management, 21(3), pp. 45-137

52-The Inter-Services Intelligence or ISI is the largest and most powerful Pakistani intelligence service.

53-Pakistan: Madrasas, Extremism and the Military.

54-Jessica Stern, "Pakistan's Jihad Culture," Foreign Affairs, November/December 2000.

55-Pakistan: Karachi's Madrasas and Violent Extremism, International Crisis Group Asia Report, No. 130, 29 March, 2007.

56-The Economist, Sep-9-2006.

57-The Telegraph, Jan 13-2010, London.

58-The Guardian, April 23-2009.

59-Daily Mail, Feb 7, 2009.

60-Telegraphs, 9 July, 2009.

19-MI5 report of August 20, 2008.

61-Intelligence and Security Committee Annual Report 2007–2008.

62-The Observer, Sunday 11 January 2009.

63-Daily Outlook Afghanistan, August 12, 2007.

64-Morning Star, 20 September 2006.

65-The Hindu, August 29-2010.

66-Belfast Telegraph. www.http://www.belfasttel.

67-Yemeni rebel leader denies seeking Shia state," Reuters, Sept. 29, 2009,

68-Daily Mirror 18 October 2010, Theresa May warns of growing threat of cyber warfare

69-Daily Telegraph—Cyber attack threat 'could be next Pearl Harbour, 18 October 2010.

70-The Times, June 18-2009.

71-Belfast Telegraph, July. 2010.

72-Daily Telegraph, May 23, 2000.

74-Guardian report, November 19, 2011.

75-Guardian reported in Nov 8, 2008.

72-Benefits of Multi-Cultural Britain: Rod Liddle, Sep, 2009.

73-Policing a Multi-Cultural Society, Edna Erez, James O. Finckenauer and Peter R. Ibarram. Police and Society, 2003, Issue No-7.

74-Britain's Multicultural Society. Nick Clegg MP, Deputy Prime Minister and Leader of the Liberal Democrats, 8 March 2011.

75-The Failure of Britain's Police: London and New York Compared. Norman Dennis. George Erdos. David Robinson. Civitas: Institute for the Study of Civil Society. London. April 2003.April 2003.

76-Police in Britain Deemed Untrustworthy Compared with Europe. Alan Travis, Guardian, 12 December, 2011.

77-Race and Racism in Britain. John Solomos. The Macmillan Press. 1992.

78-Not Easy Being British: Color, Culture and Citizenship by Tariq Modood, Runnymede Trust and Trentham Books. 93 pp. 1992

79-Policing in France and Britain. Restoring confidence locally and nationally. Report of a seminar held in London 8–9 November 2000, David Lawday, Franco-British Council British Section. Victoria Chambers. 16-18 Strutton Ground London

80-Police Accountability in the United Kingdom. Dr Rob Mawby and Dr Alan Wright, Keele University, UK. Written for the Commonwealth Human Rights Initiative. January 2005.

81-Policing and prosecution in Britain, 1750-1850. Douglas Hay, Francis G. Snyder. Clarendon Press, 1989.

82-Policing Under Fire: Ethnic Conflict and Police-Community Relations in Northern Ireland (Suny Series in New Directions in Crime and Justice Studies)

83-In Defense of Multiculturalism: Critics are attacking a Straw-man Version of Multiculturalism when they blame it for Building a Culture of Segregation. Antony Lerman. Guardian. 22 March, 2010.

84-Policing in Britain (Longman Criminology Series). Dr Les Johnston. Longman, 1999.

85-Policing in Britain: The Racial Discourse. Joe Ukemenam, Book Surge. 2007.

86-Police Faces Years of Public Disorder, Vikram Dodd. Guardian, Dec 2011.

# INDEX*



* This index was created with **TExtract**™

**H**



**I**